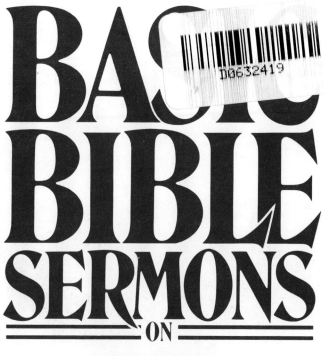

BASIC BIBLE SERMONS
ON
HOPE

David Albert Farmer

BROADMAN PRESS
NASHVILLE, TENNESSEE

Unless otherwise noted, all Scripture quotations are taken from the *Revised Standard Version of the Bible*, copyrighted 1946, 1952, © 1971, 1973.

All Scripture quotations marked (NASB) are from the *New American Standard Bible*. © The Lockman Foundation, 1960, 1962, 1963, 1968, 1971, 1972, 1973, 1975, 1977. Used by permission.

All Scripture quotations marked (GNB) are from the *Good News Bible*, the Bible in Today's English Version. Old Testament: Copyright © American Bible Society 1976; New Testament: Copyright © American Bible Society 1966, 1971, 1976. Used by permission.

All Scripture quotations marked (KJV) are from the *King James Version* of the Bible.

All Scripture quotations marked (NEB) are from *The New English Bible*. Copyright © The Delegates of the Oxford University Press and the Syndics of the Cambridge University Press, 1961, 1970. Reprinted by permission.

All Scripture quotations marked *The Jerusalem Bible* are from *The Jerusalem Bible*, copyright © 1966 by Darton, Longman and Todd, Ltd. and Doubleday and Company, Inc. Used by permission of the publisher.

Library of Congress Cataloging-in-Publication Data

Farmer, David Albert, 1954–
    Basic Bible sermons on hope / David Albert Farmer.
      p. cm.
    ISBN 0-8054-2276-5
    1. Hope—Religious aspects—Christianity—Sermons. 2. Baptists--Sermons. 3. Sermons, American. I. Title.
BV4638.F375   1991
234'.2—dc20   90-22088
                                     CIP

To my sisters and brothers in Christ
of the St. Charles Avenue Baptist Church
who have heard and critiqued my preaching
on hope and caused that hope to come
alive in me by their personal encouragement
and their devotion to Jesus Christ.

Other Books in the Basic Bible Sermons Series:

Contents

Preface

I am absolutely convinced that the greatest need among people today is hope. Progress in so many areas of human endeavor—not the least of which is life-prolonging medicines and technology—has not taken away the human tendency to fall into various kinds of hopelessness. We will never have ultimate and utter control over life. Life with its pressures and complications and our best efforts to plan, take care, and be informed inevitably goes its own surprising way. That often is not the way we want it to go, not a way we think we can bear. The problems are much broader and more widespread than simply the anxieties of our private and familial worlds. Hunger, homelessness, grief, broken homes, and the threat of war remain pervasive concerns. With the excellence of modern, world-wide newsreporting, they are daily issues which have no evident solutions. We—no matter how hard we might try—cannot correct them completely if at all. We cannot make them go away.

Right at this juncture of awareness of our finitude—individually and in human community—comes the gospel message centered in Jesus Christ: **There is hope!** Neither the world nor the expressions of evil themselves can separate any of us from the love of God which means the presence of God is with us.

The Bible is filled with such hope, and we are called to proclaim it to the glory of God.

1
Let Not Your Hearts Be Troubled

(John 14:1-3,18-19,25-27)

The fourteenth chapter of John's Gospel falls into a portion of Scripture which has been called Jesus' farewell discourse. Jesus and His disciples were facing the reality of Jesus' death and the grief and pain of separation. For the disciples there also was the fear of living without the immediate presence of their Lord and the haunting unknown—simply not knowing what the future would hold, what death meant, and how to cope without the direct guidance of a person of strength among them.

When Jesus said, "Let not your hearts be troubled" (v. 1), He wasn't suggesting that the disciples should pretend not to hurt in their loss and separation which was to come. Rather, His pastoral imperative urged them, in spite of the pain, not to be worried and upset as if all dimensions of their happiness and usefulness were coming to an end—as if through the dark clouds there could be no more light. There was reason for Jesus' friends and followers, the children of God to hope because God in the great by and by pulls together all the loose strands of tragedy, misunderstanding, and rough edges.

"As an antidote to despair Jesus bade them *believe* both *in God* and *in* himself."[1] In an ongoing relationship with our gracious God and our Lord Jesus Christ there are, ultimately, answers and—where no answers are possible—peace that surpasses understanding.

God knows when our hearts are troubled and how deeply we can despair; often these feelings come precisely because we feel Godforsaken. Right at the outset of Jesus' conversation with the hurting disciples, He pointed them not only to the providence of God in a broad sense—but also, more particularly, to God's concern for and involvement with individuals. Jesus chose a striking metaphor to describe the qualities of life in the world, where He would be going, and where His disciples, indeed—all the people of God— would someday follow Him. Jesus declared that life there would be like living in God's own house. It's a big house with many rooms: Nobody who wants to be there will be deprived of a place. Some have talked about God's big house as a "mansion." What Jesus really wanted to stress was not the impressiveness of the accommodations but the marvelous assurance of having a place to be with God[2]—in as intimate a place as God's own home—for all eternity.

There is still further assurance. God's own Son, though He too would have to walk through the valley of the shadow of death, was the One who went ahead to that big house to make sure everything was in order when the time comes for folks like us to join them there. Jesus stated that He Himself will come to take God's children home. Perhaps He referred primarily to His reappearing at the end of time, but I cannot get past the personal emphasis in the passage which suggests, to me, that Jesus' presence undergirds the child of God in death as in life. There is no separation, no abandonment, and no loneliness during the experience of death and beyond. The fact that the risen Lord has, in the power of God, overcome death means eternal life for the rest who know Him as Lord.

God's people are well taken care of. What about those left behind at a time of loss? The presence of Jesus Christ, God's Son, remains with you through the Holy Spirit. It is on Him that you will lean and in Him that you will find comfort for this day and the days ahead. This will mean peace for you. If the world has any peace to offer, it is merely external and usually transitory. This is not the kind of peace Jesus promises, not the kind He wants you to experience. The peace He offers is in His *undying* presence with you; it is that internal, deeply spiritual realization that you do not carry your weariness, fears, burdens, and grief alone.

So, in the name of Jesus Christ and because of His promises and His peace, don't be worried and upset. Don't be afraid. This one whom you love is in the loving hands of God—death passed; all struggle and pain and sickness are no more.

Notes

1. William Hull, "John" in *The Broadman Bible Commentary,* vol. 9 (Nashville: Broadman Press, 1970), 333.

2. Ibid.

2
Hope, Not Hopefulness

(1 Peter 1:3-9)

Many of us would like to feel that, in some way, sense can be made of life. As we move through the maze of *givens* and *unexpecteds* we call life, we wish we could find an assurance of some sort that what we've known and been about has meaning; further, we hope that our dear ones who come after us can chisel through the barriers to similar meaningfulness in their lives. These desires are related to what we might call "Christian hope." We want to join with those who affirm, "In Christ, Christians have hope." Do we grasp the full meaning of such Christian hope?

Some of us see Christian hope as related only to the end of time and the life beyond. Because of God's power and love, there is a "pretty good chance," we think, that "things" will all work out in the end. This perspective isn't entirely off base, but there are problems with this approach. Christian hope is more than expecting everything *finally* to come out in the wash. Christian hope has something to add to every day we live. It is both a *present reality* and an *attitude about the future*. To treat Christian hope as only a *probably*, in the future tense, is to make it merely hopefulness or wishing. *Hopefulness* is "optimism or courage in the face of bad news"[1] or else hoping but not knowing whether or not something will come to pass.

Have you ever heard a wife say something like, "I *hope* I receive flowers on my wedding anniversary"? That statement can have several meanings. It can mean, "I think there's a good chance that my husband will be considerate enough to invest in this thoughtful, much-deserved, possibly romantic, and slightly frivolous gift for me." The same statement can also mean, "There's not much of a chance that my husband will remember our wedding anniversary!" Christian hope is greater than the most optimistic of these two projections.

Christian hope is an attitude of assurance that God prepares a way and place for God's people when life as we now know it has passed. Also, Christian hope is an attitude of assurance that God is present in the lives of God's people *now* to bring meaning, wholeness, and peace through divine love "even when the world is in despair."[2] And, "Christian hope for the world is that God, and God only, can and will overcome the inhumanity of [persons] and the resulting inhumanity of their social, political, and economic structures."[3]

This kind of assurance indicates that Christian hope is inseparably intertwined with faith in God. The truths of Christian hope are as certain as the God in whom they are based. Christian hope is not a hope in circumstances, but in God Himself. It isn't a "blind yearning which reaches out of its poverty,"[4] but a vision of the present and future founded in what God has done and is doing. Though we all have our moments of doubt and uncertainty—perhaps unbelief at times—those of us who claim Jesus Christ as Lord and Savior have the right and the resources to make Christian hope the overriding attitude in our lives. In reference to Christian hope, Dale Moody writes, "Hope is to despair what faith is to doubt and love is to hate."[5]

Our lesson from 1 Peter addresses the subject of Christian hope. It is an excerpt from a first-century sermon to baptismal candidates—new persons in the faith—and it is still helpful to us today whether we happen to be new or experienced in matters of faith.

Our lesson establishes that Christian hope is known from eyes of faith; we've already alluded to this fact. It is possible for a person who has not come to faith in Christ to be attracted to our claims about hope, but the reality of hope and the power to internalize it come only to those who are in relationships with God through Jesus Christ, the risen and living Lord. Once the miracle of coming to faith occurs in our own lives—then, knowing hope for the present and the future is natural—not easy, but natural. Apart from a faith relationship with God, we are left with despair: hopelessness.

To read or hear the news on any given day is almost overwhelmingly negative. Current events suggest over and over again that care and respect for persons and our world—our environment—have been completely lost. That we continue to exist and have a place to exist is quite tenuous—especially given the fact that what we trust most are the tangibles. When these are threatened, our basis for meaning is threatened. We want to throw up our hands and ask, "What's the use?" But faith in God interrupts this line of reasoning by insisting that *in spite of* outward circumstances—personal and social—we can still have meaning in our lives, including a joy for living, because God is alive and powerful and present with any of us who will allow it. Further, whatever may happen today or tomorrow, that same God is caring for God's people. There is hope.

From her cell in a Nazi concentration camp where she was held prisoner during part of World War II for hiding Jews, Corrie ten Boom wrote—in a spirit of Christian hope:

> Time [here] is something to be waded through. I am surprised that I can adjust so well. To some things I shall never get accustomed, but on the whole I am really happy. . . . Sometimes it may be dark, but the Savior provides his light and how wonderful that is.[6]

And the apostle Paul testified in his letter to the Christians at Rome:

> For I am convinced that neither death, nor life, nor angels, nor principalities, nor things present, nor things to come, nor powers, nor height, nor depth, nor any other created thing, shall be able to separate us from the love of God, which is in Christ Jesus our Lord (Rom. 8:38-39, NASB).

My wife and I had the privilege some time ago of having a meal with Sister Joan Delaplane, one of the first Catholic women to preach in this country with papal blessing. Joan has a contagious commitment to Jesus Christ and, with it, an obvious understanding of the power of the gospel. Over dinner, she commented that the only real message Christianity has for our world is the message of hope. Her perception caught my attention.

The writer of 1 Peter directly relates Christian hope to an "inheritance" (1:4) for God's people; that inheritance, obviously, is salvation. "As the outcome of your faith you obtain the salvation of your souls" (v. 9), he wrote. Seeing "souls" saved or getting "souls" saved are overused and underdefined phrases in evangelism. The writer of 1 Peter is talking about the whole human being in the experience of salvation when he makes reference to the salvation of souls. Salvation is God's liberating us from the power of sin and self-destruction, setting us in a right relationship with God, and working in our lives to make us healthy and whole persons in all respects; it's an ongoing process. All of the best we can know in these areas of life is a mere "down payment" of that complete inheritance which is not fully realized until the world to come. We can't even imagine the bounty awaiting us when we receive the inheritance in full. So, for now, we sing, "Blessed assurance, Jesus is mine! Oh, what a foretaste of glory divine."[7]

We have difficulty trying to comprehend the value of God's gift of salvation which we as His children will someday fully inherit. Our writer picks three beautiful terms to describe salvation, which is life with God. It is life *unending* and immortal. It is life *undefiled* and pure, unstained by any moral or spiritual evil. It is life *unfading* as a flower which never loses its beauty.

Christian hope gives God's people the assurance of God's protection. Now, that is not properly interpreted the way it is popularly treated. Protection by God means that once we become children of God, we are not left to "go it alone." As we face the difficulties of life, as we struggle to make our lives more of what God wants them to be, as we deal with the continuing battle between good and evil, God is with us. God never leaves or forsakes us. Through faith, we have continual access to God's power as we attempt to handle whatever life may bring to us. Don't misunderstand me to say that God protects Christians in the sense of insulating them from all the potentially bad experiences human beings can know. That isn't true; that isn't possible.

God's protection of His people means that divine power is available to us in such a way that we have sufficient stamina and courage to be God's children in any and all circumstances. There's a big difference between saying that God will be with us, making divine resources available to us, *and* saying that God shields us. Protection in this context means that God gives us strength to be God's people in spite of any temptation or evil that may come to us.

This protection is not a deliverance from suffering, grief, and pain. God does not inflict these upon us; they are, however, realities of living as human beings in an imperfect world. God will not forsake us when these times come; we have God with us as we walk through the dark valleys, and this is an essential part of Christian hope.

First Peter was written in a time during which Christians certainly suffered because of their commitment to Christ. There were different levels of punishment inflicted upon the faithful, including death. When 1 Peter was written in the late first century, suffering for the faith meant having your life threatened if you publicly confessed Jesus Christ as Lord. Christians in that time were often faced with a dilemma, a life-and-death dilemma. All people could be required by law to bow down before the statue of the emperor (probably Domitian) and say, "Caesar is Lord." It was not uncommon for the emperors to make a divine statues for themselves. Most had not insisted upon a universal acknowledgement of this deification; however Domitian was an exception. He referred to himself as *dominus et deus,* lord and god.[8] To make such a statement as "Caesar is Lord," would be to deny Christ as Lord, yet the penalty for refusing to worship the emperor was often death. Should the Christians say it and not mean it, or refuse and leave one less Christian in the world?

God's protection has meant that He would not leave His people in the lonely hours of decision and pain. We can hardly understand that. There may be some exception here and there, but most of us don't know what it is to suffer for our faith. More than likely, no one threatened us as we made our way to worship recently. Some of you may have been threatened for trying to stay in bed or trying to participate in some sabbath recreation by someone who felt strongly that you should be in worship. (I don't have to tell you whose side I'm on.) Some persons in the world were, and others will be threatened for their association with Christians and places of Christian worship. We were stunned a few years ago when a right-wing guerrilla group in El Salvador devised a "Baptist Hit List." Two of the four persons on that list were murdered. More recently six Jesuit priests have been murdered under similar circumstances.

Enduring suffering is one thing, but do you recall what else the writer indicated about suffering in the context of Christian hope? He makes it plain there is joy in adversity when it comes because of one's faith in the Lord. He says that faithful suffering refines one's faith in God and brings honor to Him. Suffering for Christ's sake is like a refiner's fire, bringing about a purer, more precious product according to our writer. We have to be refined in this way for pure gold to result. If you have to suffer for the cause of Christ, don't despair. The end result will be a purer faith. In this way, see Christian hope as related even to suffering.

I can't think of anything more frightening than having to put my life on the line, can you? If we heed what our text says, when and if we should find ourselves in that most extreme situation, we can yet *hope*—not just that things will all end up OK but that, *then and there*, God is with us. There will be meaning in that event and perhaps even joy to be known at such a time. God grant us the courage to face life with such assurance and uphold in prayer our sisters and brothers around the world who are regularly threatened because of their Christian commitment.

Clearly, Christian hope is not our wish to be treated as something other than human; rather, it is in the midst of all that is human—the pain not excluded—that Christian hope works. Christian hope has to do with life. There is no greater power than to give life. God gave life to humanity in creating us. And an even greater display of God's power came in giving life where death had come—in raising Jesus from the death. God made hope more of a reality that day than ever before and from the raw material of shattered dreams, humiliation, and agony.

God is the basis of all our hope. Because of God's power especially displayed in the resurrection of our Lord, we boldly claim

Christian hope. With the same divine power, God brings us to true life, when we come into relationship with God. Thus,

> For us there can be no ultimate pessimism about the future—and therefore no cynicism about the value of life in the present. . . . We move not only toward the *end* but [also] toward the *fulfillment of life*— the genuinely human life which God the Creator willed for us from the beginning, and which God the Savior is already at work here and now to restore and renew in us.[9]

God raised Jesus Christ from the dead. God raised us to new life through God's living Son, Jesus Christ. We can have hope in the present and in anticipation of the future that is not mere hopefulness. It is hope, and the best is yet to be.

Notes

1. Paul D. Brewer, *Youth Affirm: The Doctrine of Man* (Nashville: Convention Press, 1977), 81.

2. Ibid.

3. Shirley Guthrie, *Christian Doctrine: Teachings of the Christian Church* (Richmond: CLC Press, 1969), 378.

4. Brewer, 95.

5. Dale Moody, *The Hope of Glory* (Grand Rapids: William B. Eerdmans, 1964), 13.

6. Corrie ten Boom, *Prison Letters* (Fort Washington, Pa.: Christian Literature Crusade, 1975), 19.

7. Fanny J. Crosby, "Blessed Assurance, Jesus Is Mine," *Baptist Hymnal* (Nashville: Convention Press, 175), 334.

8. Roland Bainton, *Christendom*, vol. 1 (New York: Harper and Row, 1966), 54.

9. Guthrie, 381.

3
Waiting for the Light to Shine

(Micah 7:1-9; John 8:12)

The sense of the predominance of evil at work all around us is at times debilitating. As best we can tell, there is little good in our lives and our world that goes unchallenged or unchecked by some evidently demonic force. In Dickens's works, "The best of times and the worst of times," is a very nice way of being able to describe one's era and circumstances, but many people can only see—and for good reason—the negatives. This is, for them, the worst of times.

The world is in bad shape—so what else is new? The world has always been in sufficiently bad shape to allow doomsdayers to have a following by talking about the inevitable and imminent end of it all. Plenty of these doomsdayers are crackpots, but some of them are sincere people who simply cannot see how the world in its condition can go on. And, as much as anything else, the basis for regarding the world as in bad shape is immorality. Every now and then, some specific instance of immorality comes along which emphasizes this fact and solidifies a view of the prevalence of ungodliness which many of us vaguely sense most of the time; some particular immorality which is a real focus on the darkness in which we feel that we live and of the little light that ever seems to break through. The "specific instance" becomes a stackpole on which we gather all our free-floating feelings and ideas making the evidence for our pessimism, for us, uncontestable.

The evidence that grabs me in regard to hopelessness of the world is the strength of organized crime and the drug-dealing subculture. I start thinking things are really bad when people expect and tolerate illegality at the highest levels in our government. I become ready to give up on the world when I have to think about nuclear weaponry. To imagine that humanity has created devices which can destroy not only our enemies but also our allies and world is chilling. To think that apocalyptic imagery no longer comes from the imaginative interpretation of biblical and literary symbols, but from real possibilities is terrifying. Disfigured beings and an earth ablaze are no longer wild ideas but what can be expected because of a device human beings have created and are willing to use under certain circumstances.

Micah is speaking for us, isn't he? What he says sounds exactly like what we sometimes say and what we read that others are saying all the time. Listen to the prophet!

> It's hopeless! I am like a hungry man who finds no fruit left on the trees and no grapes on the vines. All the grapes and all the tasty figs have been picked (Mic. 7:1, GNB).

This is the expression of prophetic lament. This is how the prophet feels as he considers the decadence of his society, the complete absence of righteous people. Pause with him a moment to feel his darkness and hopelessness. His vain search for godly people is—to him—like the seeking of a desperately hungry person who goes into an orchard after the summer fruit has been picked or into a vineyard after the grapes have been gathered; needing to find some fruit for sustenance, but finding none. It's the feeling of a hungry person who goes to one more place to find food—just knowing that when all other sources have failed—this one will not. It's a feeling of need, anticipation, and desperation. And, then, it's a feeling of frustration because the food has been there—very recently—but has been taken; somehow that's more assaulting than finding that the food is long gone or has—in fact—never been there.

Micah thought that morality and righteousness had characterized his people. These godly traits nourished the people and their society and had guided other nations. It was, after all, the responsibility of the chosen people of God to be a light to the nations in service to God, live in obedience to God's will, and live and act according to God's standards of morality. And hadn't there been times when that had been done? Certainly. But now, as Micah saw it, there were no righteous people left in Israel—none at all. The nation, thus—for Micah—was like a vineyard or an orchard with no more fruit.

From what he saw among his own people, Micah made that virtually inevitable jump to universalize. If there are no righteous people in Israel, there must be no righteous people in the world. He lamented, "The godly [ones have] perished from the earth, and there is none upright among [people]" (v. 2). What a lonely and frightening feeling. It's bad enough to feel that morality is completely absent in your family, among a group of friends, in an academic community, a city, or a political party. Maybe each of us has felt that at one time or another.

Micah may have overestimated his situation, but his conclusions were not drawn in haste. There was ample evidence all around that evil was winning over good and God in Israel and in all the world. He looked at it from this standpoint. "Where good and godly [ones] ought to be there are evil, murderous [people]."[1] As he said, "All of them lie in ambush for blood, each hunts his brother with a dragnet."[2]

> To lie in wait for blood is to be willing to commit murder if need be to get what one wants. This was the common law of the city. Everybody was capable of it. There was no such thing as trust and loyalty. Greed and lust were such that [people] would trap and ensnare their own [siblings] if the price was right.[3]

Wait a minute! Is this Micah or a daily newspaper? What about all these spying charges in recent years? People have sold out the safety and security of the rest of us to those who might do us harm by making available highly classified information *for a price*—and not just a little slipup in many instances but careers of spying.

What about that company a couple of years back who knowingly manufactured defective pacemakers and acted—quite consciously—to cover up the problem? People's lives were on the line when those faulty devices simply stopped functioning. It wasn't just a season's worth of products; the malproduction had gone on for five years before the word leaked out. If the price is right, let sisters and brothers in the human family die to keep the profits up.

What do you say about those who know—as all of us now do—that drinking alcohol and driving kills people, most of them innocent. People know this and drive on our streets and in our neighborhoods anyway.

Micah zooms in, now, on the power people—the rulers and the upper-class types.

> Their hands are upon what is evil, to do it diligently; the prince and the judge ask for a bribe, and the great man utters the evil desire of his soul; thus they weave it together. The best of them is like a briar, the most upright of them a thorn hedge (vv. 3-4).

The leaders of the people of Israel weren't even casual in their evil deeds; they sought diligently—with eagerness and preparation—to do wrong, such as selling justice and doing it openly, without shame. They were so willing to do wrong that they went public with the news that they could be bought. As a group, they planned together and then wove their evil into society. The best of them would hurt persons as would a brier on the stem of a lovely flower or thorns in a row of hedges.

Now Micah didn't think this could go on and on, but rather than thinking his people, their whole society, would finally self-destruct, he saw some light, only a ray but some light. He doesn't elaborate at this point in his oracle. He only mentions it: "The day of their watchmen, of their punishment, has come; now their confusion is at hand" (v. 4). Micah believed that in a state of evil, people and nations would ultimately fail. The prophet believed with all his heart that those sold out to evil and not to God would be plundered by others who lived for evil. After such a confrontation, there would be "confusion"—total disorganization of life. When this came, it would mean light for the nation as a whole because evil would have been defeated.

There was no righteousness among the leaders; that was clear. Micah also knew that there was no righteousness among families and friends. He warned:

> Put no trust in a neighbor, have no confidence in a friend; guard the doors of your mouth from her who lies in your bosom; for the son treats the father with contempt, the daughter rises up against her mother, the daughter-in-law against her mother-in-law; a man's enemies are the men of his own house (vv. 5-6).

As he looked around he saw that even normal family relationships and friendships had disintegrated; there was no respect and no trust.

Micah found a connection between the absence of trust and immorality. If we are not willing to be responsible enough to be trustworthy—as individuals, as a society—then we evidently bear no need for moral behavior. Can you trust me to be who I say I am? Can you trust me to try acting in your best interest rather than in a self-centered manner? If not, you can't trust me in any other way because I have proven that I am not standing on the foundation for moral action. I have said by my lack of trustworthiness that you don't matter to me.

Talk about darkness! Huckleberry Finn wrestled with darkness in his society and his own darkness as well. In Huck's Southern world, a high crime was helping a runaway slave which he had done for Jim. Huck became torn because of the prevailing attitudes of those who had reared him from a proslavery perspective, the "dirty abolitionists," and his own friendship with Jim, the slave, who had sacrificed for him, taken risks for him, and had been through all kinds of adventures with him up and down the "Big River," the mighty Mississippi. Later Huck sang:

> I am waitin' for the light to shine
> I am waitin' for the light to shine
> I have lived in the darkness for so long
> I'm waitin' for the light to shine.[4]

You've been there, haven't you? One being engulfed in darkness, darkness all around but "waitin' for the light to shine." It's your personal darkness. You're a long way from home, and loneliness won't go away. You're in a required course that you can't pass, and it won't go away. There is that guilt for some long-ago failure that won't let light in. There is the burning grief that will not let you rest. There's a health problem that threatens your life. There is something that keeps you from being faithful to God.

You're in darkness, but you're "waitin' for the light to shine." That's faith. To believe that the light *will shine* when all you know is darkness—that's faith.

It was hopeful; it was a matter of faith that Micah used an image of an orchard or vineyard where there was no fruit, but where there could be new growth in season. Listen to this prophetic liturgy,[5] his hymn about the victory of faith.[6]

> But as for me, I will look to the Lord, I will wait for the God of my salvation; my God will hear me. Rejoice not over me, O my enemy; when I fall, I shall rise; when I sit in darkness, the Lord will be a light to me. . . . [God] will bring me forth to the light; I shall behold [God's] deliverance (vv. 7-9).

> Who is a God like [you], pardoning iniquity and passing over transgression for the remnant of [your] inheritance? You do not retain [your] anger for ever because [you] delight in steadfast love. [You] will again have compassion upon us, [you] will tread our iniquities under foot. [You] will cast all our sins into the depths of the sea (vv. 18-20).

Israel may be fallen now, but she shall certainly rise. Darkness has overtaken her temporarily, but God is her light, the light over which no darkness can be victorious. In all that God does, redemption is God's aim; therefore, God acts to forgive those who have failed and those who struggle but who do not wish to remain in darkness.

That is why we do not have to live as people without hope. That is why we need not pronounce doom on ourselves, our society, and our world. With faith in God and God's goodness, there is hope. We may be "waitin' for the light to shine," but, there is already some light, isn't there? Jesus said: "I am the light of the world; [the one] who follows me will not walk in darkness, but will have the light of life" (John 8:12). Amen.

Notes

1. Elmo Scoggin, "Micah" in *The Broadman Bible Commentary,* vol. 7 (Nashville: Broadman Press, 1972), 225.

2. Ralph Smith, in *Word Biblical Commentary,* vol. 32 (Waco: Word, 1984), 54.

3. Scoggin, 225.

4. "Waitin' for the Light to Shine," by Roger Miller. Copyright © 1985 Tree Publishing Co., Inc. All Rights Reserved. International Copyright Secured.

5. Smith, 55.

6. Scoggin, 226.

4
Obedience and Suffering

(Isaiah 50:4-9; Luke 19:28-40)

One of the lies we tell children in our culture is that if they are "good" and do what is "right" then they will not be hurt. This principle is true at first, when stated as a way to get them to keep hands off hot stoves, but we never get around to tell them that the application is limited. No, we let them go on thinking that the same principle applies in broader relational and spiritual spheres as well. We let them believe that if they are honest and tell the truth, good will always come to them. When they become older, we lead them to believe that if they speak out and stand up for what is morally acceptable, both heaven *and* earth will smile on them. We tell them that if they will take our advice about which *good* paths to follow, they will be able to move through life virtually unscathed by forces of evil and persons who see life differently than they do; even by their enemies. We tell them in the church that if they will *always* do what God wants them to do, they will be shielded by God's protective care.

So we lie to our children, and one of the reasons we lie to them about this matter in particular is that, though we know better, we don't want to believe differently. We keep wanting to believe that if we simply do the right thing and act in a Christian manner, everything will be all right. Whatever would hurt or frighten us will go away. While our reluctance to deal squarely with the facts is understandable, we are not doing ourselves or our children any favors with our coverups.

Because we lie to them, children become adolescents and then adults who are naive enough to believe in this kind of fairy-tale

world. Many of us were those children who became adults still trying to live in make-believe. Somebody told us—somebody we
trusted—that if we would be careful to do the right things, we'd be
happy, be safe, prosper, and not get hurt. When the negative, unfortunate, painful, and tragic invaded our lives, the only conclusion we
could draw was that we had *done* something wrong, but for the life of
us we didn't know what it was. You know that lonely feeling, don't
you?

"What is it? What did I do to deserve what is happening to
me?" After the exhausting inventory of personal performance is
taken time after agonizing time, and we find no great lapses of moral
degradation or sinful rebellion, we are left with no recourse but to
turn on ourselves as inherently evil, those who have told us the lies,
or even God for not delivering what we mistakenly believe has been
promised. By this point in our lives, we are rarely capable of ques-
tioning the formula we have memorized: "Good deeds keep bad
things away from us and bring only good to us." Isn't that it? "Good
deeds keep bad things away from us and bring only good to us."

For those who mature emotionally and spiritually without that
kind of catastrophe, a kind of crisis of suffering which blows away
our formula leaving nothing in its place, there is still a painful process of observing that "being good" and "doing good" will not
always bring us good. There is no honest argument for pursuing a
moral way of living, yes a Christlike way of living based on some
presumption that good living wards off bad. Life just doesn't work
that way. We may be meticulous in doing what is ethically appropriate and Christlike in most every situation that confronts us only to
be overtaken by events and circumstances that are anything but
good. Some reward, huh?

At some point we have to come to the vital realization that suffering is not given out by the supernatural forces in the universe
which have chosen us as unsuspecting and unfortunate victims.
Suffering is common to humanity, and a good deal of suffering
which we must endure has nothing to do with our religious commitments or the lack of them. As Walt Whitman worded it in his poem
of universal human experience, "Song of Myself": "Agonies are one

of my changes of garments."[1] Being good people, being God's obedient people, does not remove us from the plight of being human—with *all* its joys and *all* its pitfalls.

Suffering is no confirmation of obedience to God. A human being with a conscience and a normal range of emotion is equipped to suffer. There is suffering that comes to us precisely because we are God's people trying to do good in God's world. We can rail and rebel against it, but it is part and parcel of life. So do not let suffering lead us to some false and proud sense of martyrdom. Most of us cringe at the thought of suffering. We may not run from it, but we won't beg for it either. We are surprised, then, when we come upon a person who actually enjoys suffering, tries for it, and interprets much of life from that perspective. This person uses the unfortunate as some kind of a reminder or badge which signifies "hurting for God." No one has yet asked that suffering be enjoyed.

Listen, children, adolescents, and adults: Living the good life is no guarantee that your way will be free of encounter with pain and difficulty. Being a devout Christian will not always bring enough good to outweigh the bad for you. Rather, through a careful study of the foundations of Christianity and—more powerfully—through the consistent living out of a relationship with God, we will find more often than not a correlation between obedience to God and suffering than we will find between obedience to God and success.

When Jesus proceeded into Jerusalem a few days before His death, He believed that He was placing His life at risk because He was being obedient to God, not something new for this young man, but a way He had lived consistently. And yet, what awaited Him there in Jerusalem? What was in store for this man who honestly only did good deeds for God's sake? Nothing but suffering. Nothing but suffering. Some reward, huh?

In the life and death of Jesus of Nazareth we see the epitome of the connection between obedience to God and suffering. We have taught, and we have desperately wanted to believe that these were mutually exclusive; at times, we have even needed to believe it. But it isn't true. Obedience and suffering are wed in lives like Jesus' life.

And as He is our Lord and our example, our obedience to God will in some way be wed to suffering too.

I'm not suggesting that if you are God's person you should be prepared *in case* suffering should come your way; I'm not suggesting that you brace yourself to prevent a possible brush with the unexpected. What I'm saying for all of us to hear is that obedience to God *means* suffering. Count on it. It may be that those who oppose God will actually turn on us, bringing us that kind of suffering; I'd say this is likely if we ever roam out of protected Christian environments. Or, the suffering we can expect may mean that as obedient children of God our hearts grow tender like God's heart and thus connect us to those who struggle and lose so much and hurt so often that we suffer with them. Whitman, again, without any intention of describing this kind of Christian suffering did a powerful job of it anyway when he said: "I do not ask the wounded person how he feels. I become the wounded person."[2] Jesus in His obedience to God knew those kinds of suffering: the pain of direct attack and the pain of identification. Jesus, no doubt, experienced *all* kinds of suffering.

When the prophet Isaiah wrote about the seemingly anonymous Servant of the Lord with whom Jesus would later be identified, Isaiah didn't overlook the suffering in the life of this person whose experience either foreshadowed or hauntingly foretold the plight of the one we name as our Lord. Isaiah, speaking for this Suffering Servant, said: "I bared my back to those who beat me. I did not stop them when they insulted me, when they pulled out the hairs of my beard and spit in my face" (Isa. 50:6, GNB). As Jesus rode the donkey into Jerusalem, this was precisely the fate that awaited Him: taunting, beating, being spit upon, and more. Yes, more. The prophet set this account of suffering in a longer monologue which gave some explanation for why and how the Servant of the Lord endured such suffering. He explained in the Servant's words:

> The Lord has given me understanding, and I have not rebelled or turned way from him. The Sovereign Lord gives me help. I brace my-

self to endure [my enemies]. I know that I will not be disgraced, for God is near (vv. 5,7-8, GNB).

It is clear that there is one reason for the Servant's suffering—because he is an obedient servant of God. That's also the only reason Jesus suffered, isn't it? In our Old Testament lesson, in the testimony of the Suffering Servant, there are a number of truths through confession which tell us a good deal about the suffering of God's people—even this select one among all God's children.

The Suffering Servant does not look for suffering, but he does not run from it as if suffering is beneath him or not his lot. He is brave enough to face it. There are reasons for his bravery. In the midst of the suffering, he does not make the most common mistake of all, which is turning away from God in trying times. By continuing to cling to God in his trials, in his suffering, the Servant of the Lord has strength because of God's nearness and also because of the understanding that comes in spite of crisis. This is not to suggest that there are good reasons for the suffering of God's people. *Understanding* does not imply this. There *are* reasons that God's people suffer, but they are not good reasons. This realization is itself a part of the understanding which comes to suffering people like you and me who decide to continue clinging to God in spite of the pain which we are certain we don't deserve.

The basis of suffering is action. Living as a child of God is a life chock-full of challenging tasks and risks. It is anything but a life of genteel passivity. Yes, to be God's people we have to act. Being Christian means involvement in causes and lives not at the top of the preferred list. What kind of motley crew would Jesus die for? Being Christian means doing. There is suffering for God's obedient children because we are willing to act and try to do the right thing, according to God's will in a world that, to say the least, isn't particularly attune to God's concerns.

There is suffering for God's obedient children because serving God is a matter of faith, and faith means that there are moments when we must act and launch out to try to do good without all the information we might have desired. Indeed, faith is a particular kind of risk. On the paths of faith, there is suffering for God's obedient children because God's people finally become committed to serving God above all else; consequences become secondary considerations. It had to be that way for Jesus. He could not have focused on the likelihood of His death, or He would never have entered Jerusalem when He did. However, the timing was right; he went at Passover when many of the Israelites were gathered together to think about the great God of deliverance and liberation. This was the best opportunity to tell—in a way that only He had or could ever tell—of the extravagance of God's love. Instead, Jesus focused on His task, His opportunity to be *the* Servant of God. He did not go into Jerusalem like an abused pup expecting every move to be a beating; He rode into Jerusalem like a King! And without saying a word, people knew it. They threw their coats on the ground to make a path for someone with the bearings of royalty, and without prompting they began to yell out: "Blessed is the king who comes in the name of the Lord! Peace in heaven and glory in the highest!" (Luke 19:38, NIV).

The Pharisees were repulsed, and they insisted that He rebuke those who went so far as to associate Him with the Lord God, but Jesus said: "I tell you, if they keep quiet, the stones will cry out" (v. 40, NIV). The one who had suffered for God and the one who was going to suffer more than He may have known, still could hold His head high in obedience—not in pride, but in obedience. People knew that He was God's Son. Everything about Him proclaimed it.

So my sisters and brothers in this community of suffering, fight on in your obedience to God—not fighting to destroy your enemies, fighting only for the privilege of obedience and honor of being called God's servant; whatever the consequences may be. Amen.

Notes

1. In *The Norton Anthology of American Literature,* 2nd ed. vol. 1 (New York: Norton & Co., 1985), 2014.
2. Ibid.

5
Sharing the Journey

(Psalm 18:1-3,31-33,49; Lamentations 3:19-24;
Philippians 4:10-13)

One of the traits we obviously value most in ourselves and others is *independence.* Few accomplishments in America are more admired than pulling yourself up by your own bootstraps and rising to the level of virtual independence through personal effort and ingenuity alone. In fact, we probably consider this as our ideal.

The people we seem to admire most are those who are least dependent on others—the foreman more than the person on the assembly line, the administrator more than the administrative assistant, or the owner of the business more than those who work for her. This adoration of independence goes beyond the working world.

In the academic world we admire the student who needs the least amount of help in—and outside—the classroom or who makes it without a tutor more than the one who needs the tutor. I've heard parents make remarks indicating that they most admire the child who makes it on his own—without their help—the fastest or does the best, the quickest outside the nest. Our love of independence—because we think that independence means strength—causes us to have higher regard for those who appear to make it through life without the help of a psychiatrist, psychologist or pastoral counselor than for those who do have this need and do something about it. Our high regard for independence has national and international implications, too. We want to be the greatest power in the world, not "beholdin'" to anybody. We think we're superior to all the other nations that the thought of an apology when we're wrong is taken as an affront. We take the need to say, "We're sorry. We've made a mistake," as a sign of weakness and thus a lack of independence.

This love of independence is all around us. It even affects our spiritual lives; perhaps we should say that it *especially* affects our spiritual lives. Somehow we've let the drive for independence convince us that depending upon God is not good—that really strong, mature Christians learn to make it to a large extent on their own.

Independence is good, if it means doing or being what you *can be* in your own strength and through your own efforts. There is certainly unhealthy dependence. Independence is not good, however, if it means that we come to believe that we are totally sufficient in every way unto ourselves and can do all we need to do in every way in our own strength. We begin to believe that we don't need others at all, and that may be a step or two away from deciding that we can make it without God's help, too. I'm not talking about those who separate themselves from the church, having decided that they don't need God anymore. I'm talking today about those of us in the church who are trying to live as if we don't need God's help in our day-to-day achievements and struggles, as if spiritual maturity means going it alone and merely "checking in" with God from time to time.

There is not a time in our lives—not even a day—when we can be at our best without the active presence of God, not only guiding us but also strengthening us for the tasks we undertake. Refusing or neglecting to receive the strength God is willing to give us is *not* spiritual maturity; it is spiritual carelessness. Spiritual maturity *never* means independence from God. Theodore Parker Ferris said, "You don't grow out of this sense of dependence upon God; you grow up into it."[1]

Throughout the Psalms there are references to dependence upon God and His help. One such psalm is Psalm 18. This passage avoids two unhealthy extremes: (1) on the one end of the continuum, it avoids the suggestion of passive dependence—the state of assuming that God will do everything, even what we should be using our own abilities—strengthened by God, of course—to accomplish; (2) it also avoids the suggestion of independence from God.

It is a poem or hymn for worship, and verses 1-3 are the invocation. The poet comes right to the point: "I love thee, O Lord, my strength" (v. 1). In this sentence, we find the confession of faith that this person makes in the one who strengthens and empowers him. We know without reading further that this writer believes he has not and does not have to face life and its tasks in *his* strength alone. God helps him meet the demands of life, and he knows it. He doesn't feel any pressure to be fiercely independent. He doesn't feel that if he reaches out for help from God he becomes a weakling. He knows that *the* sign of weakness and carelessness is in trying to live life without the guidance and strength of the One who made life, the only one who has real strength to offer.

The poet, in this invocation, pictured God as his rock—his foundation for living. He saw God as his protector. We can see that this poet is a warrior, probably King David. David—as is the case with us—obviously was not shielded from all the effects of evil, but as God's child he could not be overcome ultimately by evil. The place he could put his trust in life—the place he could really put his weight down—was with God. God is the only worthy foundation for living, but not a passive foundation, a wistful wisher of goodwill. God is *actively* at work in our lives to help us do His will and meet the demands and challenges of being human without being overtaken by the evil in the world.

In verse 31, the psalmist asks, "For who is God, but the Lord? And who is a rock, except our God?" Make no mistake about it! This God is the one God, the God of Israel; He is both the foundation of our being and—if we are wise—the source of our guidance and the one in whom we trust.

The psalmist was convinced that the God whom he praised in worship was the God who girded him with strength. The help he needed to live as God's person was so real it was like armor; it was like something he wore, and, therefore, his way was safe. Evil, no matter how great it was and no matter in what form it came, could not ultimately overcome him.

Sometimes, I think, when we come for worship, we want the event to be something like a pep rally or a transfusion. We look at it as something that will get us going for a few more days of service. It's as if we leave God at our public or private place of worship.

Then, we see ourselves as going out to face the world on our own. This is incorrect. We don't leave God anywhere. God is with us, not just watching what happens to us but actively involved—if we permit it—in our dealing with all facets of life. God is with us offering us strength to use in bearing the burdens, facing the disappointments, serving wherever we are led, and doing the tasks necessary to serve the Lord well. We don't have to go it alone, and—in truth—spiritually, we really can't. We need God and the strength God gives like a warrior needed armor for battle.

David said that "He made my feet like hind's feet, and set me secure on the heights" (v. 33). That is, God gave him a firm and careful stance in the insecure places of life, like a doe who is sure-footed on uneven and unpredictable terrain. It's the same picture the psalmist had in mind in verse 36: "Thou didst give a wide place for my steps under me, and my feet did not slip." David was thinking of battle situations, but we can have the same assurance in the situations we face. The situations may change, but God is the same.

There is much insecurity and vulnerability about our lives. There are many times when we think we're going to slip and fall because of the terrain, situations that come to us over which we have absolutely no control, and even because of bad situations that we bring upon ourselves. The ground becomes very uncertain along the way. The causes may differ, but the results are the same. We think we're going to fall; we don't know if we can keep standing. You know exactly what that feels like, don't you?

To assure that we keep standing, when in our strength we will surely fall, we need God's strength, too. So why refuse it? Reaching out for help or an arm to lean on is not weakness. Weakness is refusing to reach for help when we need it, and we do need it daily in the Christian life. Weakness is falling because we won't take the help that is available to us, and God's extra measure of strength is always available to us.

The writer of the Book of Lamentations was not too proud to ask for God's help:

Remember my affliction and my bitterness [he said to God]. . . . My soul continually thinks of it and is bowed down within me. But this I call to mind, and therefore I have hope: The steadfast love of the Lord never ceases (3:19-22).

George Fox, founder of the Quakers, related the moment that this reality first dawned upon him. He said,

> . . . when all my hopes . . . in all men were gone, so that I had nothing outwardly to help me, nor could tell what to do, then, Oh then, I heard a voice which said, "There is one, even Christ Jesus, that can speak to thy condition," and when I heard it my heart did leap for joy.[2]

Let us rejoice today that strength is available to us right now for facing whatever life has brought us, and that strength is in Christ Jesus. Claim it! Let it work in you!

Paul claimed it and wrote about it for the benefit of the Christians in Philippi. In Philippians 4:13, Paul said triumphantly, "I can do all things in him who strengthens me." He wasn't talking in abstractions or generalities. He was talking about real and hard experiences of living. He had been persecuted. He had been hungry. He was in prison when this letter was written. Eventually he would die because of his unswerving commitment to Jesus Christ. If he had tried to face all these situations in his own strength, he would never have made it with his emotional and spiritual health intact. Because he saw the real source of strength through God in Christ, was willing to reach out for it, and let it work in him, he had real life, abundant life, in spite of innumerable hardships—hardships that would have defeated those of us who think that it's a sign of weakness to depend on God and the power He offers us so that we can be victorious people in the world.

The bottom line is this: Without God's strength we do not have the power to face life, much less live it. Life as it was meant to be is not some pronounced spiritual independence which tries to become, for all practical purposes, self-sufficiency. Life as it was meant to be is a shared journey—day-by-day living in the close company and companionship of God. The shared journey is not simply to enjoy the presence of God, though that is a joy and an added benefit; it is, rather, an intimate relationship in which each person gives and takes and wherein we receive—for the willingness to receive it—strength to live.

I urge you to claim this strength because I believe we all need it. But how can we get it? When Paul says, "All things I am strong to do through the One who strengthens me," he is thinking of the result of intimate relationship. He is able to draw strength from Christ because Christ intimately shares life with him. Christ is able to empower him and make him strong enough to deal with the rough places and the tragedies of life because Paul is willing to receive the strength from outside himself. This essential power is not something that can be claimed by one who occasionally bumps into God; it can only result from a continuing, dynamic relationship with God. That's it! Strength from God is not a neatly wrapped gift or something we can receive on demand. It is an outgrowth and inevitable result of depending upon God as we share the journey of life day by day with God. Don't you need that?

Notes

1. Theodore Parker Ferris, "Depending on God," *This Is the Day* (Dublin, N.H.: Yankee Press, 1980), 11.

2. Hugh T. Kerr and John M. Mulder, eds. *Conversions* (Grand Rapids: William B. Eerdmans, 1983), 43.

6
Our Very Present Help

(Psalm 46)

We join you today in this painful event as friends who share in your grief and disbelief. (This is a sermon following the death of a loved one.) We share your sense of deep loss and the profound wish that there might have been some other way. We have no answers or explanations; we, like you, are inclined to search for ways to understand, but we have all already discovered that such a search is in vain. And still—without answers, explanations, or ways to grasp what has happened—we stand alongside each of you with the hope and confidence in Jesus Christ that the last word has not been spoken. Even in this situation of what feels to us like finality in the extreme, the God of life will not let it be. The God who gives life—physically and spiritually—has already taken the one you love into His divine arms and welcomed her into her heavenly home.

We understand all too well that you nearest her remain in a state of confusion, heavyhearted and bereaved, lonely and confused. Of course, how could it be any other way? What I have to offer today is a simple reminder that the God who loves and has provided for her eternally, also loves you and is ready to help you bear the heavy load. This is the abiding message of the Christian faith and only basis through which we can face life's grim realities with a sense of hopefulness intact. God loves you, abides with you, and will not forsake you in these moments and in the days of readjustment and reorientation which are ahead for you.

This surely is the message of the psalm 46. Where could we find stronger words of comfort? These are words especially for you today.

Not only are the psalmist's words beautifully rendered and reflective of profound insight, but also the very logic provides a pastoral word of comfort and inspiration. The writer begins with the full force of theological reality, a statement of religious confession and assurance which gives order and hope to his life and to the whole human family. This is the beginning point. This is the lens through which we view world events and the more immediate circumstances affecting our lives. Any other point of departure, any other frame of reference, will distort not only how we see, but also how we hope. The psalmist began with God, and so must we.

Not just any god, mind you, but with the one true God, the creating, redeeming, and loving God. The God on whom His people may depend; and with only a little bit of experience in our uncertain and many times cruel world, we see that this is the God on whom we *must* depend. "God is our refuge and strength, A very present help in trouble" (Ps. 46:1). Therefore, let us come to grips with our grief, anger, fear, and loneliness which result from this untimely death by looking first to and through such a God as this, the God to whom Jesus also pointed. Because of His own reliance upon God and because God was so much in Him, Jesus could say, "Come to me, all who labor and are heavy laden, and I will give you rest. . . . rest for your souls" (Matt. 11:28,30).

The psalmist's assessment of God does stir us to reach out to God because God is reaching out to us in a living presence that helps us fend off enemies from without and enemies from within. God is our refuge; in relationship with God, we may take shelter from outward attack such as a tragedy over which we have absolutely no control. Oh, there will come a time to step out of the shelter and take on the enemy, but even then God will be with us because God, too, is our strength. The psalmist's summary of theological affirmation is that God is a present help in trouble; come what may, God's presence is what we need to cope and keep on searching for the divine meaning in life. Again, this is where we begin, not with the trouble.

The trouble is real, and God never ask us to ignore it; that would be disastrous. However, in spite of trouble, the psalmist still draws our attention godward. As an example of trouble, the psalmist recalled a personal experience—perhaps the most horrifying experience he could have imagined: an earthquake. Even in that time when he feared for his own life amid death and destruction all around, he could still affirm that God was his refuge and strength.

What you have been living through for the last several days is like a personal and emotional earthquake—with much of your joy and stability threatened and even dying. Finding peace and courage to rebuild will not be easy. You can find some courage and encouragement that you're not up against it all alone. In both the material and emotional rebuilding and healing, the Lord of hosts is with you; the God of Jacob is your refuge.

7
Not Made with Hands

(2 Corinthians 5:1-5)

I'm glad that we share a belief that one of the ways God speaks to us is through the Holy Scriptures, and furthermore, that part of what God says to us in the Bible is there for our comfort. Our passage from the apostle Paul is a practical and theological reflection in which many people do find comfort.

Paul was not always in the mood for comfort, but he manages here in spite of himself. He told the Corinthians, at some other place, that he was better at building up than he was at tearing down. This brief passage is part of that reality.

Paul had a keen eye for what mattered, and much with which we worry day by day really doesn't matter. He could look beyond the limitations of our earthly existence and set the value of life here and now in the context of eternity.

One fact about which he was certain is that there is more to human life than the body in which we live, during our years on earth. This body is important and essential in the way God has created us. We won't overlook that, and we don't want to. Paul was quick to remind us that when this body fails—and it will—it's not the end of us by any means. "For we know that if the earthly tent we live in is destroyed, we have a building from God, a house not made with hands, eternal in the heavens" (v. 1).

The *"tent,"* when set up properly and well cared for, can last and give those who use it protection and enjoyment, but there are no delusions about its durability. A tent is something human-made, not permanent; we could not live there long. Paul contrasts a tent with a *house that God builds*—a heavenly, eternal home. This eternal home with God is promised to all who are children of God. We want it, and we need it. "Here indeed we groan, and long to put on our heavenly dwelling" (v. 2).

Life lived in relationship with God is so rich and full. When we begin to understand just how wonderful it is, we don't want to lose out on such life—ever, and we don't have to. God's children don't lose out on it. Instead, what happens is that, in God's vast plan, mortality is "swallowed up by life" (v. 4). The essence of who one is is transformed into fullness in the heavenly realms—no more weaknesses or limitations.

It's hard to believe, isn't it? "[The One] who has prepared us for this very thing is God, who has given us the Spirit as a guarantee" (v. 5). Through the Holy Spirit of God, there are constant renewals in our lives and in the lives of many people we know, and these take place in an imperfect world. If this goes on here in this life and we can know a sense of renewal and resurrection in this life, how much greater the transformation God has waiting for God's children in heaven! The best of life in the present is only a foretaste of all that God has for God's own.

Dear friends, your loved one and our friend has moved out of his tent and into a most elegant heavenly home, a heavenly body in which he can celebrate his wholeness even as he joins the celestial choirs singing praise to God. He has begun to receive the gifts of eternity; he is in a new home, not a home made with hands but a home made by God. Though separated from you for a time, he is well-cared for. After all, to be away from the body as we know it is, for God's children, to be "at home with the Lord" (v. 8). And so he is. Amen.

8
Never Drifting from Hope

(Colossians 1:21-29; 2 Chronicles 7:11-15)

In Alice Walker's novel, *The Color Purple*, Celie—who had been through more than her share of abuse and grief—writes a strange letter to Nettie, her missionary sister, who has been reported dead. Celie refers to the telegram she received from the U.S. Department of Defense. She wrote that she had heard that Nettie and her family had gone down in a ship struck by a German mine. She linked the bad news to the fact that life is a terrible ordeal.

I said it was a strange letter; it was written to someone who had been reported dead. We may think of such a letter as an acceptable way to express an especially private grief, or we could see it as denial of painful reality. We might see it, though, as hopeful. Celie will not shut down—on the basis of a piece of paper—the hope that Nettie is, somehow, still alive. The "system" had never worked for her; instead, it had only brought her pain—over and over again. There was no basis for her to trust it now. Her emotional response to this situation could be nothing more than grasping at straws; maybe it was just her intuition, or was it hope   an internal spark that, even when the breath is knocked out of her by the fear of loss, won't go out?

Some time later, Celie is rocking on her front porch when an unfamiliar car speeds up the road and stops in her yard. Nettie, whom she had not seen in more than thirty years and long since reported dead, steps out. At this *glorious* moment, you want to shout for joy with Celie.

We live in a world that is so massive, so tentative, and often so tragic that we have a hard time putting much stock in hope of any kind. In fact, we may be living in such a time that the fullness of hope—from the Christian perspective—is all but impossible; for us, hope can be little more than wishful thinking at best. Maybe that's all a "secularized hope" could ever be since a great deal of the aptness and believability of hope has to do with the object of our hope. Then the question, "In what do we base our hope?" or "In whom do we ground our hope?" becomes absolutely essential.

Let's say that we occasionally wonder to ourselves if there are any real possibilities for a "better world." None of the rose-colored glasses stuff, but honestly and realistically, is the world going to worsen, stay about where it is from generation to generation, or somehow get to be better off? That's a justified concern. There probably are numerous answers to the related questions we would raise in regard to our concern. The way we ask the questions has a great deal to do with what kind of answers we can expect. Again, in what do we base our hope or in whom do we ground our hope? In other words, in what context are we raising the questions about possibilities for a better world?

If we ask from a strictly secular point of view, if we wonder whether or not humanity—on its own—will ever do much better than it has done or is doing to make the world a better place, we don't have many reasons to be optimistic about improvement; though we may live in an age in which there are a few more reasons for optimism than we have had since the ending of the Vietnam War.

However, if we ask about a better world theologically and wonder in a Christian context—being careful to leave aside all false optimism—I think we come out at a completely different place. Christian hope as far as the world is concerned has to do with what *God* can do with and through us, and that changes the picture entirely. Further, Christian hope moves well beyond wishful thinking and inner sparks to assurances. God has said that the world *can be* a better place.

King Solomon had prayed for forgiveness for the people of Israel who had sinned against God, and God's response was:

> . . . if my people who are called by my name humble themselves, and pray and seek my face, and turn from their wicked ways, then I will hear from heaven, and will forgive their sin and heal their land (2 Chron. 7:14).

In the same chapter out of which our New Testament lesson is taken, Paul "has a long Christological hymn that ascribes both creation and preservation" of the world to Jesus Christ.[1] As the Colossian hymn sings it:

> He is the image of the invisible God, the first-born of all creation; for in him all things were created, in heaven and on earth, visible and invisible, whether thrones or dominions or principalities or authorities—all things were created through him and for him. He is before all things, and in him all things hold together (1:15-17).

Dale Moody has called attention to German theologian Karl Heim who pointed out that Paul's "dynamic view of the universe" here is "most congenial to belief in a living God who creates the world continuously anew."[2] If these scriptural and contemporary analyses are anywhere near correct, there *are* solid reasons for expecting that the world can be a better place.

What kind of world would be better? A world with less war and more international community is desired—where justice prevails and homelessness and hunger are not forced on anyone. A better world would be a place in which cancer and AIDS would be cured and young people can justifiably look to the future as bright. A better world would be a place in which the elderly are affirmed and never made to feel no longer needed and the environment is respected and cared for as every other God-given gift.

This is where Christian hope differs from wishful thinking or mere hopefulness. The gift has been promised, and it *will be* delivered. We don't know when, and we don't know if it will be gradually or suddenly; we cannot control or manipulate God. Certainly there are some contingencies. The more we can open ourselves to the will of God, the greater chance there will be that the world will begin improving around us. If that could spread and multiply—think about the world impact!

In spite of these principles which we may very well believe *in theory*, mustering hope in this world and from where many of us sit today is an overpowering challenge. We may feel like David in the movie, *Every Time We Say Goodbye*. He was a young American soldier serving in the British armed forces in Jerusalem during the early 1940's, when threats of invasion by Hitler's troops hung heavy there. Sarah, the young Jewish woman with whom he was falling in love, asked David to tell her more about his father who was a Presbyterian minister in the United States. David began by describing his father as a good man whom he was bound to disappoint; Sarah wonders why.

David explains: "Because my father believes that God is just and merciful and that the world can be remade in His image."

Sarah asked, "And you don't?"

After a pause, David confesses, "I think God has a lot to answer for. And I don't think He can change the world—not much anyway."

David may have been onto something. There are always new stories which seem to contradict hope for a better world. Still, as hard as hope may be for us, hope in the Christian heart is treated in much of the New Testament as a foregone conclusion. That is true of our New Testament lesson today.

There are two related and important phrases in what Paul wrote to the Colossian Christians: ". . . never letting yourselves drift away from the hope promised by the Good News" (1:23 *The Jerusalem Bible*) and ". . . Christ among you, your hope of glory" (v. 27, *The Jerusalem Bible*). These are not synonymous by any means, but they do support one another.

The first phrase is directly related to reconciliation in relationship to God which the Colossians had experienced—what we all experience when we come into a right relationship with God. Paul reminds them of the "before" and "after." He called to their attention that there was a time. Before their reconciliation with God and when they were busily involved in doing evil deeds, it was a time when they were "estranged and hostile in mind" (v. 21). They were estranged from God and many of the people around them. They undoubtedly felt isolated, alone, and as if they didn't belong.[3]

We all know these kinds of feelings, and we know them too well—isolation, loneliness, and no sense of belonging. Even on "this side" of reconciliation with God, these feelings still creep into our lives, but before meaningful relationship with God, they were surely heightened, leaving us with an overpowering sense of hope-lessness about life and the world. Of course, living at odds with God, the center and the foundation of our being, creates a sense of alienation rather that belonging; we feel rejected rather than loved.[4] This surely has something to do with the "hostility" to which Paul also refers. Because of our separation from God, perhaps we see God as the enemy; there is a "deep distrust of others, and a desire to hurt or destoy them."[5]

Paul asks the Colossians, and he asks us to remember what that was like—especially in contrast with the recollection of what having been reconciled with God has meant. *Now* Jesus Christ "has recon-ciled you, by his death and in the mortal body" (v. 22, *The Jerusalem Bible*). Paul challenges the feeling of being unloved. Jesus Christ has brought about the opportunity of being made right with God, by His living out *in the flesh* the love of God though it meant His own suffering and death on our behalf. When we are confronted with these realities, it's much more difficult for us to pout and nurse our anger—off by ourselves in some lonely corner of life. That is the ba-sis of being made right with God because it begins at once to dis-solve both our sense of hopelessness and the emptiness of alienation that drives us and keeps us in the foreign land of hatred. Celie said in the midst of her early troubles and despair as long as she had God, she had somebody. That changes everything, doesn't it? When we know we've got "somebody along"—somebody who listens and cares with us for the long haul, our outlook is unavoid-ably changed.

A right relationship with God becomes a possibility, and if we enter into this relationship—persevering in spite of the tendency to fall back into our old ways and standing "firm on the solid base of the faith" (v. 23, *The Jerusalem Bible*)—we are transformed. Instead of being estranged and hostile, our lives are characterized, according to Paul, as "holy, pure and blameless" (v. 22, *The Jerusalem Bible*). These qualities are goals for faithful and forgiven children of God, and together these terms describe persons who have been recon-ciled to God as those who are free from reproach[6] in terms of moral-ity and integrity. No longer trapped by evil, we are free to receive the love of God and live as whole and God-directed folk. Trying to live in obedience to God, trying to live in ways that bring honor to God, there should be no basis for reproach either from God or from people who know us. The basis for the kind of perseverance which makes such living possible is hope, hope that things really are the way God says they are; we must never let ourselves "drift away from the hope promised by the good news, which [we] have heard, which has been preached to the whole human race" (v. 23, *The Jerusalem Bible*). Not that everybody literally has heard, but that the message is *for* all people. In Christ, all people have the right to be hopeful about their lives and about their world. We're a long way from realizing that, though, aren't we?

But that's a good deal of what we're to be about as God's people—helping to make this kind of world a reality because God didn't promise magic in place of hard work. Along with our work to make people's lives worth living, we spread the good news. We have to find our way to participate in what Paul said was his "divine office." We must find our way to put people in touch with the Christ hope, our way

> to make the word of God fully known, the mystery hidden for ages and generations but now made manifest to [God's] saints. To them God chose to make known how great among the Gentiles are the riches of the glory of this mystery, which is Christ in you, the hope of glory. Him we proclaim, warning every [person] and teaching every [person] in all wisdom, that we may present every [person] mature in Christ (vv. 25-28).

The proclamation of such hope must become our passion, and we will say with Paul: "For this I toil, striving with all the energy which [God] mightily inspires within me" (v. 29).

Contemporary with Paul and the early expansion of the Christian church were pagan religious groups known as "mystery religions." Paul is speaking to them and to the Colossians who were a little too enamored with the practices of the mystery religions.

> These mystery religions promised salvation to those persons who joined them and learned the secret rituals and doctrines that were

supposed to give them spiritual power. . . . Paul used the word "mystery," but gave it a new turn. Instead of using the term to mean that which was hidden from all but a few, he employed it to refer to that which God had revealed openly.[7]

However, it remained a mystery in the sense that what God was offering to all people could only be fully understood by those who received it relationally in Jesus Christ. As Paul put it: "Christ among you, your hope of glory" (v. 27, *The Jerusalem Bible*), the second of the key phrases in our passage.

As members of [Christ's] body they had his life within them. They therefore had a sure hope that they would share in that fullness of glory yet to be displayed on the day of "the revealing of the [children] of God."[8]

Hope in the present for God's people is undeniably attached to the future hope that all the riches promised for that time and place "out there" have already begun to trickle into our lives right now, even into this defective and painful world where hope for the day is hard to come by.

Don't drift away from the hope that is rightfully yours. Believe it! Celebrate it! Christ is in you, and that means nothing in your present or future can separate you from the love and the presence of the living God.

Notes

1. Dale Moody, *The Word of Truth* (Grand Rapids: William B. Eerdmans, 1981), 140.

2. Ibid.

3. Harold Songer, *Colossians: Christ Above All* (Nashville: Convention Press, 1973), 43.

4. Ibid.

5. Ibid.

6. Peter O'Brien, "Colossians, Philemon" in *Word Biblical Commentary*, vol. 44 (Waco: Word, 1982), 68.

7. Songer, 530.

8. O'Brien, 870.

9
God Our Strength

(Habakkuk 3:2-6,17-19; 1 Corinthians 2:1-5)

When the pressing times of life come and our coping capacities are not sufficient, where do we turn? Or when we need support with energy merely to make sense of life day by day, on whom do we call? The answer you would expect to hear from a Christian pulpit— especially on a Sunday morning—is "God." And most of us would want to give that answer, but are we really convinced that God is our strength? I think many of us have had evidences of God as strength in our lives, and we likely wish we could appropriate this reality more consistently. So how do we come to the point of living in such a way as to find our strength in the Lord? Well, coming to the point has something to do with the degree to which we believe that God can be our strength; this fact becomes a conclusion by which we live.

A principle way by which we come to conclusions is through a type of ongoing inner conversation. Our understanding of God, for example, is rarely shaped in any major way by a single reading, service, conversation, or experience. Rather, we take what we glean from all of these, and process our "hypotheses" over periods of time; certainly thinking about them and maybe testing them in verbal exchange or even action. The real testing ground of our thoughts about God, though, is the inner conversation with God as we contemplate the validity of certain assumptions. In this sense, we *do* theology, and we are involved in the ongoing process of faith development. It's certainly a "nonexact science." If we're appreciative of free thinking and rethinking, we can grow by the rather continual testing of positions we have held. We're evidently trying in this pro-

cess to move to some conclusion which will give us greater understanding, greater assurance, or at least will allow us to survive for a
time. Our lives are finally shaped by the few conclusions—the
absolutes—we may be able to call them, which we are able to reach
by what amounts to integration of many strands of thought.

Our Old Testament lesson takes us into one of these inner con-
versations with God. Though the form is polished and poetic because Habakkuk had prepared this prayer for public worship, the
content or gist of this prayer is the same as the inner dialogue and
the searching conversation we often have with God as we look for
what we can hold onto.

There's something about coming into God's presence—
regardless of how comfortably we may slip into conversation with
God, certainly unconscious at times—which often makes us "test
the waters" a bit. That's justified, since there is more to God than we
know. There can be this sense of being acquainted and yet unac-
quainted with God. It has nothing to do with how God relates to us
as if God intended to "keep us guessing" about where we stand.
God has made that clear through the revelation of Himself in Jesus
Christ. Even so, there is more to God than we can comprehend so
our approach is cautious—a feeling out of things. John Baillie caught
the motivation for this attitude in the opening lines of a prayer he
penned in *A Diary of Private Prayer:*

> Almighty and eternal God,
> Thou art hidden from my sight:
> Thou art beyond the understanding of my mind:
> Thy thoughts are not as my thoughts:
> Thy ways are past finding out.[1]

I suppose when honesty prompts us to address the issue of
God's vastness, we are asking questions like: Have we really known
You, God? Have we understood You at all? How reliable are the
statements we have heard made about you (and people say a lot
about you, God)? It's natural to raise these kinds of questions. Habakkuk had heard God called a God of deliverance, and he had also
heard some unspeakable acts attributed to God and were called

God's judgment. So Habakkuk prayed, "O Lord, I have heard the report of thee, and thy work, O Lord, do I fear" (Hab. 3:2).

In addition to expressing Habakkuk's wariness in coming before God, this excerpt and in the whole Book of Habukkuk reveal an underlying concern. Habakkuk wants to know why wickedness seems to swallow up justice in the world if God is any kind of God at all. God's vastness and all that has been attributed to God caused Habakkuk to fear God, not primarily in the sense of facing possible harm at God's hand, although this wasn't unheard of in the prophet's day and time, but with sufficient mystery to want to come into God's presence and to this subject with reverent caution.

Habakkuk continues his dialogue with God by appealing to the side of God he had heard about and wanted most to believe, which he hoped against hope was the true nature of God. And, not surprising to us, it was the attribute of God which caused people to call God merciful.

Habakkuk considers the times in which he lives to be turbulent and troublesome for himself and his people. That's what he means by the phrase, "in the midst of the years" (v. 2b). "In the midst of the years" calls God's attention to Habakkuk's own day—filled with difficulty and need. Destruction and violence mar his community; strife and contention arise. Nations rage and devour those weaker than they. The arrogant rule, and the poor suffer. False gods are worshiped throughout the world.[2] Thus, Habakkuk prays for God's mercy. He also prays, if God's wrath is somehow evoked by what he and his people are doing, let God remember mercy.

We now know that we do not have to plead with God for mercy; but for his time, Habakkuk was a very forward-thinking prophet. He dared to hope that God's mercy could prevail, though actions of human beings certainly could justify, in the reasoning of the day, acts of angry judgment on God's part. The prophet thinks he is justified in seeing God as merciful and, thus, asking for mercy based on the dramatic display of God's role as deliverer; this was no pipe dream. God had been known in history to act as deliverer. This was nowhere more clearly seen, as Habukkuk understood, than in the exodus—the leading of God's people away from Egyptian bondage.

So Habakkuk calls up this image in his prayer as he works toward having his assumption become fact for him. God is pictured as a warrior.[3] God is marching from the region of Sinai toward Edom—as God did at the exodus when the Israelites were delivered at the Red Sea. The implications in this vision are that God can again show mercy and deliver the people, and that—as has been done—the enemies of God's people will be overcome by God.

When God moved to deliver the people, God's "glory covered the heavens, and the earth was full of his praise" (v. 3) writes Habakkuk. Of course, this depends on where you were and who you were. The Israelites may have noticed God's glory in the parting of the Red Sea, but the Egyptians—as you can imagine—weren't nearly as impressed with this "God" that the Israelites were thanking as the water closed in on their heads. For the purposes of Habakkuk's vision, God as deliverer shines when people are liberated; and when persons are liberated, the earth itself fills up with praise for Him because there is harmony with the intention of creation itself. Nature is involved in the praise.

Light dominates the sight of God who comes to deliver the people. Rays, like rays of the sun, shone forth from divine hands, but while the light tells of God's splendor and might, it also veils the extent of God's power (v. 4). Even when God has done mighty deeds and we are praising Him for His greatness, there is much more that we have not seen; and we cannot see because we cannot know all of God. Habakkuk was not out of line in approaching God with reverent caution; that remains our basis of approaching God today.

It follows, for Habakkuk, that if God's people are liberated, then what has kept them from freedom will be destroyed. As God the warrior comes to deliver them, pestilence comes ahead, and plague follows behind as tools of destruction to those who oppose God (v. 5). *Pestilence* seems to refer to disease, and *plague* evidently alludes to disasters of nature. The Egyptians had experienced these as severely as they had refused to let God's people go.

God the warrior, in Habakkuk's prayer-vision, now takes a position from which He examines the conditions in all the world: "He stood and measured the earth." And as God looked, nations shook; people became fearful because of what might come to them as a result of this warrior's judgment. The earth itself feared such acts of judgment: the mountains scatter or crumble, and the hills sink. The earth quakes in fear of the judgment of God because God has been said to have so acted in the past; God's "ways were as of old" (v. 6), literally, God's "ways are everlasting."[4]

If this is how God acts, fear is inappropriate; utter terror is called for. Habakkuk is never able to put this out of his mind. His prayer is very honest and genuine. His problem is our problem: What to do with all that is attibuted to God? Is God a God of mercy as many have said? Is He a God of judgment as others insist? Both? Without the benefit of God's revelation in Christ, Habakkuk moves into the realm of hope and faith and comes, in verses 17-19, to a powerful affirmation of his faith in God's mercy.

His vision is over. His rehearsal of the dramatic acts of God as warrior has been offered to God and the people who worshiped with Habakkuk. Back into his present things have not changed. He and His people are still "in the midst of the years"—still in need, still despairing.

But, somehow in spite of all this, Habakkuk, still in worship and dialogue with God, breaks out into song. His song is a magnificent song of trust, [5] and the basis for his desire to find his strength in the Lord.

Though [and *though* may very well be the key word here] the fig tree does not blossom, nor fruit be on the vines, the produce of the olive fail and the field yield no food, the flock be cut off from the fold and there be no herd in the stalls, yet will I rejoice in the Lord, I will joy in the God of my salvation (vv. 17-18).

What if the difficulties continue? What if Habakkuk tells his people there is no relief in sight? What if our crops are destroyed and we end up without basics like figs and grapes and olives or no food at all? That's a drastic thought and extreme. He is not proposing some aesthetic lack or being deprived of some frill. He proposes, in his inner reasoning, the possibility of being without a very basic

food; doing without food can change everything—attitudes, perceptions, and commitments. For further complications, what if our
flocks are lost and livestock is taken by a group presumed to be
God's agents of judgment? Easier said than done to be sure, but at
least Habakkuk said it with conviction and sincerity. Even though all
these come to pass, he confesses, "I will rejoice in the Lord, I will joy
in the God of my salvation" (v. 18). His response is as extreme as the
possibilities he entertains.

In the midst of horrid circumstances tainted with implication
that God somehow caused the pain as a means of judgment, Habakkuk is singing, and his song says he will rejoice in the Lord
anyway—not in what has happened, but in the Lord. His song says
he will be joyful—not in the pain caused by the difficulties, but in
God, the source, of his salvation. That, dear friends, is an amazing
statement of confidence in God, and it is only in this way that he can
hope to lean upon God for strength. God has the power to be the
source of strength; that is established as fact for Habakkuk. God is
capable of acting in mercy even toward disobedient children; that,
too, is established as fact in Habakkuk's mind. Whatever else might
be said or thought of God, these facts settle for Habakkuk that God
is the real source of strength in life's strained, confusing, and painful times: "God, the Lord, is my strength."

"God, the Lord is my strength." Habakkuk concludes that God
is his strength because, in addition to God's mercy, Habakkuk finds
the feeling of safety and security in his relationship with God: "he
makes my feet like hinds' feet, he makes me tread upon my high
places" (v. 18). The hind, in the deer family, was known for its speed
and surefootedness. Habakkuk felt secure in the face of insecurity
because of what he knew that God could do for people. He felt this
security as a hind was secure in its ability to leap rocks and streams
and to move with agility through precarious mountain passages. In
the heights, no harm could come to the hind, and in the same way,
Habakkuk felt safe because God sustained his life as if in high
places.

Can we come near such a confidence in God's power? Remember Paul's writing reminds us that our confidence in God cannot rest

on human wisdom—our ability to figure how and why—but must rest in the fact of God's power itself. (See 1 Cor. 2:5.) With all the questions and reservations in his mind, Habakkuk still comes to this moving confession: "God, the Lord, is my strength." It is not unlike the eloquent conclusion reached by the nineteenth-century poet, John Greenleaf Whittier. In his poem, "The Eternal Goodness," Whittier wrote:

> I see the wrong that round me lies,
>   I feel the guilt within;
> I hear, with groan and travail-cries,
>   The world confess its sin.
>
> Yet, in the maddening maze of things,
>   And tossed by storm and flood,
> To one fixed trust my spirit clings;
>   I know that God is good!
>
> I know not what the future hath
>   Of marvel or surprise,
> Assured alone that life and death
>   His mercy underlies.
>
> And if my heart and flesh are weak
>   To bear an untried pain,
> The bruis'ed reed He will not break,
>   But strengthen and sustain.[6]

God, the Lord, is your strength, too—and mine. If we believe it, we will believe it because of God's mercy—a fact about which we will have become convinced through inner conversation with God. But, we will always have to believe it in spite of our reservations and confusions about the why of evil in the world and our own pain. Even so, let it be.

> Though the fig tree does not blossom . . .
>   and there be no herd in the stalls,
>   yet I will rejoice in the Lord,

I will joy in the God of my salvation.

God, the Lord, is my strength (Hab. 3:17–19).

Notes

1. John Baillie, *A Diary of Private Prayer* (New York: Charles Scribner's Sons, 1949), 21.

2. Elizabeth Achtemeier, *Nahum-Malachi* (Atlanta: John Knox Press, 1986), 57.

3. Ralph Smith, "Micah-Malachi" in *Word Biblical Commentary*, vol. 32 (Waco: Word, 1984), 115.

4. Achtemeier, 57.

5. Ibid.

6. Roy J. Cook, comp. *One Hundred and One Famous Poems* (Chicago: Contemporary Books, 1958), 105-7.

10
The Rich Harvest

(Luke 10:1-12,17-20; Proverbs 10:5)

"The Lord appointed seventy [people], and sent them on ahead of him, two by two, into every town and place where he himself was about to come" (Luke 10:1). What we have in this verse of Scripture is a picture of missions and ministry to which we are all called; it pictures women and men committed to Jesus and His cause going ahead of or preparing the way for the Lord and touching lives in the spirit of the Christ who will be coming to them for a personal visitation. We often wonder what it is we're supposed to say to people whom we believe do not know Jesus Christ; indeed, the issue of a way to witness for thinking Christians is a troublesome one for many of us. Maybe we've stumbled across a strand of Holy Scripture which will help us here.

Our task as witnesses of and for Jesus Christ—at home and abroad, as we say—is to go, with other people of faith, to every place where Jesus is about to come. Jesus is ready to come to any place where persons have been prepared to meet Him.

In our secular age, we are concerned about the validity of the ideal of life in Christ for all people that we are hesitant to believe anybody wants anything to do with Christ or Christianity. Jesus says this is not the problem at all. Jesus knew that there would always be persons receptive to the truth of a God who loved them and was reaching out to give them life. No, the problem is not the slim pickings out there. Jesus said: "The harvest is plentiful, but the laborers are few; pray therefore the Lord of the harvest to send out laborers into [the] harvest" (v. 2).

"The mission of the seventy" as some summarize this passage

does not refer to an exclusive group called out to special service. The seventy people who went out ahead of Jesus were the first—with the possible exception of John the Baptist and the apostles—to do what all Christians are called to do: prepare a way for the Lord in the hearts of those who have not found the reality of life in Jesus Christ. I'm not talking about tactics which resemble accosting people rather than caring for them. I'm talking about kindness, courtesy, and genuine interest in the well-being of others. I'm talking about being understanding, forgiving, compassionate, and encouraging. I'm talking about showing others the spirit of Jesus Christ alive and at work in us—imperfect folk who have nonetheless found life through having made a permanent place for Jesus in their hearts. I'm talking about caring for people in very natural and comfortable ways and places long before any words of witness ever need to be spoken. There are people dying for that kind of affirmation and hope. Indeed, the "harvest is plentiful."

It is time for the rich harvest which Jesus has promised. Then, why not go out to reap the harvest? Because "the laborers are few." Pray for more laborers, but be careful when you "pray . . . the Lord of the harvest to send out laborers into [the] harvest" because in order for those prayers to be answered according to God's will, more laborers will have to be found; and we are the only extra laborers there are. If God puts out that call for more laborers, here we are. If any new workers go, we will have to be with them, and the assignment is demanding.

Getting close to people and opening ourselves up for genuine care and an honest witness to our own source of strength requires that we make ourselves vulnerable, and that means we can get hurt. Some people will not be receptive even to the love of God, and they may take out their anger or their frustrations on anyone who seems to possess it. This is why Jesus said: "Go your way; behold, I send you out as lambs in the midst of wolves" (v. 3). Margaret Clarkson was precisely on target with regard to this less-than-glamorous dimension of Christian service when she wrote the words to a hymn as if Jesus were speaking to those of us considering the possibility of making ourselves available to go and prepare the way for Him. Clarkson heard Jesus saying to us,

> So send I you to labor unrewarded,
>   To serve unpaid, unloved, unsought, unknown,
> To bear rebuke, to suffer scorn and scoffing—
>   So send I you to toil for Me alone.
>
> So send I you to hearts made hard by hatred,
>   To eyes made blind because they will not see,
> To spend, though it be blood, to spend and spare not—
>   So send I you to taste of Calvary.[1]

Even though we may treat the subject rather casually—not even fully committed to the idea—in Jesus' mind involvement in people's lives to prepare them for His personal visitation is an ongoing and urgent task which explains His strange-sounding instructions: "Carry no purse, no bag, no sandals; and salute no one on the road" (v. 4). Clarence Jordan translates these words of Jesus in our vernacular: "Don't carry a suitcase or a wallet or shoes. And don't stop and gab with everybody you meet" (*The Cottonpatch Version of Luke and Acts*). Malcolm Tolbert explains that these seventy people who first lived the mission and ministry which we too must carry out "will travel completely divested of provisions. . . . They will not have the security of possessing enough even for one future meal."[2] This says something not only about the urgency of the mission in that there will not be time to stop, pack bags, get traveler's checks, and plan meals, but also this business of traveling without provisions will continue to remind us of our complete reliance on Jesus as the source of supply for all our needs.

I remember telling one of my teaching colleagues in Switzerland about my elaborate plans for getting together a good system of retirement income and how much monthly we needed to put away in order to do what we want to do in our senior adult years. I was in my early thirties; he was fifty and much less materialistic than I found myself at that point in life. I thought I had found an understanding ear; instead he laughed and said in high-pitched disbelief, "My goodness, David. Jesus will have come back by then." That wasn't what I expected to hear! That comment, which I often remember, helps keep me reminded of the uselessness of materialism and the calling I share with you, today and every day, to be—first and foremost—on mission for Jesus Christ.

Being preoccupied with our own comfort, present and future, generally sidetracked with things of the world is so easy; in fact, for many of us, it is the most natural posture. Against it, we see how much the kingdom of God—the God Movement[3] in the world— pales in comparison to our ever increasing list of priorities which has nothing to do with serving and honoring God. The truth is that in success-oriented America and American Christianity, we can barely identify—if at all—with the idea of putting God and God's will first, regardless of the consequences. Back to Margaret Clarkson's hymn again. Is it possible to hear Jesus making these kinds of demands on His laborers?

> So send I you to leave your life's ambition,
>   To die to dear desire, self-will resign,
> To labor long, and love where men revile you—
>   So send I you to lose your life in Mine.[4]

The gospel doesn't offer any apologies about the demands it makes of us; there is a no-nonsense clarity with which the rewards and the burdens of being one of Jesus' people are presented. In our New Testament Lesson, for example, Jesus isn't mincing any words, and there is clearly no way we can comply with Jesus' call to us unless doing the will of God is an all-consuming desire. Certainly the writer of Proverbs is correct in his practical wisdom that reminds us: "A [child] who gathers in summer is prudent, but a [child] who sleeps in harvest brings shame" (Prov. 10:5).

Reaping the harvest in this ancient farming culture was a family responsibility; everybody in the household who was able had a part in it, including children who were old enough to work. Sleeping through the time of harvest was considered shameful. Similarly, it is God's will that we all participate in the rich harvest out there, so that we are ignoring our family responsibility if we ignore the right time for the harvest, and the right time, dear friends, is now.

The urgency of Jesus' call, however, doesn't mask the fact that there is a practicality about Jesus' instructions to the initial seventy missionaries and to us:

> When you go into a home, first greet them by wishing them peace. If a truly peaceful [person] is there, your peace will take root; . . . if there isn't, it will bounce back on you. . . . And to whatever city you go—and they accept you—eat what's set before you and heal the sick in the town. And keep telling them, "The God Movement is confronting you." But if you go to a city and they *won't* accept you, go out on the main streets and say, "We are shaking off every particle of dust from your city that's sticking to our feet. But let this be clear to you: *the God Movement is here*" (Luke 10:5-6,8-11, *The Cottonpatch Version of Luke and Acts*).

When Jesus talks of "a truly peaceful [person]," He is speaking of someone sympathetic to the cause—not just nice, accommodating folks. So on our mission if we come upon persons also concerned about the urgency of serving God, the peace of God will create a bond between us—whether or not we are culturally matched and speak the same language. When we come upon those who are not sympathetic to the cause, there will be no way for the peace of God to bless or unite. We're bound to come across some of both, so Jesus gives a little more instruction.

If we come upon those who are open to our message, that's all we're looking for. There is nothing more to expect so we are not to be concerned about the quality of hospitality, and we are not concerned about whether their religious expression matches ours; our preoccupation is to be with our mission.[5] We graciously receive what is given us; we receive such people as they are, and we do all that we are equipped to do to serve them in Jesus' name, whether that is healing their sick or, as one Baptist congregation does, repairing the homes of the elderly.[6]

When we come upon those who are not open to what we are trying to do for Jesus' sake, politely disinterested, and rigorously and rudely opposed to the news we bear and the service we offer in

Jesus' name, well, Jesus had some advice on what to do in this situation, too. We tell any of the dissenters who will listen that we are wiping the very dust from our feet that got on us while coming to them. That sounds pretty nasty, but it is intended to be a "dramatization of the fact that [these people are] under God's judgment."[7] We don't like the word "judgment," but without trying to soft-soap it, we can understand it to mean that there are losses for those who reject the love of God—not a particularly pleasant message, but an honest one. The present and the future are different than they would otherwise have been for those who become a part of the God Movement.

Well, the seventy went out and did what Jesus asked them to do according to his directions, and they experienced some notable successes. Luke reports that when they came back from their initial mission, they were joyful and said to Jesus:

> "Sir, even the most devilish ones gave in to us when we approached them in your name." He said to them, "Yes, and I saw the whole satanic structure smashed like a bolt of lightning from the sky. Look here, I've given you the ability to trample on 'snakes and scorpions,' and on the power-structure of the opposition, and nothing will be able to stop you. But don't get all hepped up just because the devilish guys gave in to you; instead you should be happy that you're enrolled in a spiritual cause" (Luke 10:17–20, *The Cottonpatch Version of Luke and Acts*).

Jesus was saying to persons who saw the gospel successfully at work—through numerical increase and dramatic effect on teller and hearer—that they had to keep such success in perspective. Yes, the gospel works; it changes lives. However, this kind of change is *always* effected through the power of God—not through the power of the teller of the good news. He or she is always, at most, a catalyst for the work of God. If we forget this, we will certainly mistake God's power as our own, and we will begin to take personally the appreciation which changed people express. We will come to believe that people owe us for our efforts, and religious scandals will be repeated time and again.

What should really thrill us is not our own success stories of how *we* helped the gospel to function in the lives of people who had been sold to evil, but the more foundational reality: that the gospel of Jesus Christ first changed us and the power of God grasped our souls and gave us hope in a hopeless world. This alone should make us willing laborers for the demanding harvest which Jesus called "plentiful."

Can you think of any task which promises to pay you greater dividends than this ministry of the harvest and laboring to prepare people to receive all that God wants for them? There is no greater calling, no greater opportunity than to be laborers together in the fields "white unto harvest." People out there desperately need us on their way to finding God in Jesus Christ. The voice we hear calling us to them is the voice of Jesus. Let's go!

Notes

1. E. Margaret Clarkson, "So Send I You," stanzas 1 and 4, *Hymns for the Living Church* (Carol Stream: Hope, 1974), 481.

2. Malcolm Tolbert, "Luke" in *The Broadman Bible Commentary,* vol. 9 (Nashville: Broadman Press, 1970), 90.

3. Clarence Jordan's term for the kingdom of God.

4. Clarkson, 481.

5. Tolbert, 91.

6. *The American Baptist,* July/August 1989, 29.

7. Tolbert, 91.

11
God's Promises Kept

(Joshua 21:43-45; Acts 13:26-33)

The issue is trust. Can we trust God? That is the writer's concern. It is our concern. We live in a world that makes us ask that question, and asking it does not brand us as either disobedient or sinful. In fact, we probably ought to ask it now and then.

We are taught to put our lives into God's hands, but there is much about God that even the most devout fail to understand. Infrequently we, many of us anyway, are driven to ask whether or not God is trustworthy. Our question may be silent, but we ask it nonetheless.

There are a variety of places to look for evidences of God's trustworthiness. Our Old Testament writer preferred to look to God's promises—to see if they had been kept. The result is a story of the promised land in retrospect.

The biblical books which we classify as the "Former Prophets"—Joshua, Judges, 1 and 2 Samuel, and 1 and 2 Kings—offer a theological/historical look at the Israelites in Palestine, from the death of Moses until the fall of Jerusalem in 587 B.C. The Book of Joshua, the first in the set, tells the story of the Israelites under the leadership, obviously, of Joshua, Moses' immediate successor. Focusing largely on the conquest of the people in the land of Canaan and how the land came to be divided among the Israelites, it is a "bloody" book, detailing battle after battle. Such war, however, is defended as the will of God. That is, there was war because the Israelites were trying to take the land God had promised them. Again, Israel's view on the matter was grounded in what she took to be God's promise and was tied in the idea of covenant relationship with God. Simply put, a covenant was an agreement in which two parties made certain commitments to each other and in so doing obligated themselves to specified actions.

It all went back to Abram's call: "The Lord said to Abram, 'Leave your native land, your relatives, and your father's home, and go to a country that I am going to show you'" (Gen. 12:1, GNB). Abram—later called Abraham—did just that. He took his wife, nephew, followers, and possessions and went to the land of Canaan. At a place called Shechem in Canaan, God appeared to Abram and said, "This is the country that I am going to give to your descendants" (12:7, GNB). God made a promise.

The promise was repeated on several occasions. For example, the free but frustrated Israelites who were delivered under the leadership of Moses out of Egypt in what turned out to be desert wanderings, God promised:

> Obey everything that I have commanded you today. Then you will be able to cross the river and occupy the land that you are about to enter. And you will live a long time in the rich and fertile land that the Lord promised to give your ancestors and their descendants (Deut. 11:8-9, GNB).

At the beginning of the Book of Joshua, we hear the promise again. The Lord is speaking to Joshua with these instructions:

> Go over this Jordan [River], you and all this people, into the land which I am giving to them, to the people of Israel. Every place that the sole of your foot will tread upon I have given to you, as I promised to Moses (Josh. 1:2-3).

Without any wavering, the Israelites believed that they had come to the land that was rightfully theirs. They had waited and waited. Generation after generation had passed on. There had been much suffering and death on the way to being where they believed God had led them, and now they were prepared to use whatever means necessary to claim the reward of their obedience.

> Never did [Israel] claim to deserve it, nor even to own it. The land was Yahweh's; only [God's] doing battle on Israel's behalf had assured her

possession of [the land]. It was within [God's] designs, so Israel rea-
soned, that her warfare was conducted.[1]

Israel's warfare was conducted in Canaan—and with success. The
writer of Joshua reports, "The people of Israel divided the land as
the Lord had commanded Moses" (Josh. 14:5, GNB). In their eyes,
this was not a new plan at all.

In addition to the basic promise of the land, somewhere along
the way (Deut. 3:20) God had also promised the ability to enjoy the
promised land. As the writer of Joshua recalled:

> The Lord gave them peace throughout the land, just as he had prom-
> ised their ancestors. Not one of all their enemies had been able to
> stand against them, because the Lord gave the Israelites the victory
> over all their enemies (21:44, GNB).

On these bases, the writer comes to the answer to his question
about whether or not God keeps promises. What we have here is a
moving affirmation and confession of faith in God who is absolutely
trustworthy. The writer looked back, having scrutinized the evidence, and said with assurance: "The Lord kept every one of the
promises that he had made to the people of Israel" (v. 45, GNB). The
Lord kept every one of the promises made to the people of Israel.

Let's be clear about what God actually promises. To say, "God
said," before some word gives that word, lesson, or instruction more
credence than it would otherwise have. It is not hard to see this principle at work, and for all kinds of reasons it is much abused. We try
to put into God's mouth what we want to hear, and the message we
put there may range from promises of our own prosperity all the
way to damnation of our enemies or people we just don't happen to
care much about. When we are not able to own our self-motivation
for making a given decision or choosing a certain course of action,
we, as people of God, often blame our choices on God; though we
may express such pietistically. We become all too careless in using
phrases like "God told me" and "God led me." We end up blaming
all kinds of crazy things on God.

I have been concerned for some time at how in contemporary

American Protestant preaching and, in particular, the high-profile media preaching, that a relationship with God is increasingly tied to the promise of material blessing. The suggestion is made (sometimes it is much more than a suggestion) that if one will give his or her all to God, riches and all manner of success and safety in general will come to that person. And the preachers who make such promises are always filling their explanations with assurances such as: "God has shown me" and "God laid it on my heart to tell you." The truth is that more of a case can be made for the person of God having a tough row to hoe since those who sell out to God will always be in conflict with the ways of the world. Christianity is not accommodation of religion to cultural norms or expectations. Christianity is radical obedience to God in the way Jesus showed us. He died because of His commitment to God. Radical love as God defined it put Jesus in conflict with the political and religious establishment that they did away with Him. There was no promise from God, His Heavenly Father, which prevented that. When we align ourselves with the way Jesus did things and what Jesus taught, our politics, economics, and personal relationships as well as our institutional commitments will not be much like what prevails in our world; there can be any number of unpleasant reactions from those around us. God has never promised that the world which largely opposes God's way will make it particularly easy on God's people.

Let's not forget, though, that God does speak to us. God does lead us. God makes promises to those who enter into covenant relationships with Him. We have almost an innate awareness of God's promises because God's promises are tied to helping us be God's people. God's promises, then, are tied to our needs, not our extravagances. We need leadership. We need God's presence. We need a place to be God's people. God promises all of these.

We have the promise of a clear revelation of God through God's self-revelation, the living Lord Jesus Christ. In our Lord is our leadership for living. This is the concern of our New Testament lesson. Paul is preaching to some people in Antioch of Pisidia when he says that he and his comissionaries there have come to bring this good news: "What God promised our ancestors he would do, he has now done for us, who are their descendants, by raising Jesus to life " (Acts 13:33, GNB).

God had spoken through Jesus and intended to continue. God had promised the Messiah, an instrument of salvation, and God's raising Jesus from the dead was not only God's strongest affirmation that Jesus was the one, but also the unmistakable evidence that God made good on the promise.

We have the promise of God's presence. Near the end of Luke's Gospel, these words of Jesus are recorded:

"I send the promise of my Father upon you; . . . stay in [Jerusalem] until you are clothed with power from on high" (Luke 24:49). This promise was that after Jesus' followers no longer had Him physically with them, they would not be alone. God would still be with them in the Holy Spirit who is the presence of God. We can claim that promise, too. We know it is fulfilled.

In Romans, Paul picks up that Old Testament promise of the promised land, and he says:

> The promise to Abraham and his descendants, that they should in-
> herit the world, did not come through the law but through the righ-
> teousness of faith. . . . in order that the promise may rest on grace and
> be guaranteed to all his descendants—not only to the adherents of the
> law but also to those who share the faith of Abraham (Rom. 4:13,16).

I hardly think we should arm ourselves and go to take over Canaan as our promised land—much less the whole world as Paul had come to view it. Could it be that God has promised to faithful people a place where they can be faithful and we can be God's people without interruption of government, culture, or those who are faithless? Perhaps this is the promised land for us. And, properly understood, this is not a contradiction of the reality we have already faced—that Christianity stands in conflict with the world. We have a new understanding of the promised land, shaped by the Old Testament revelation and perspective of Jesus to help us see more clearly now what it is that God promises us a place to be the people of God. The promised land for which we long is not a utopian Christian society in which things go well for us and the non-Christians have a rough go of it. Rather, it is a place within society; namely the community of faith—the church. Though we continue to try and bring Jesus and His message to bear upon our world, even its negative response does not take away the reality that we, the people of God, have the promise of a way and place where we can be all that God wills for us to be.

Indeed, God is still making promises and keeping them. For those of us who are willing to enter into relationship with God through Jesus Christ, our Lord, promises are made which speak of meeting our needs and bringing us life. Our God, whom we find to be absolutely trustworthy, makes good on every one.

Note

1. James West King, *Introduction to the Old Testament* (New York: The Macmillan Co., 1971), 170.

12
In Search of Our Homeland

(Hebrews 11; Genesis 12:1-5)

A friend of the family amuses her loved ones with a predictable announcement when she's up against frustration and perplexity: "This world is not my home," she says, "I'm just a passin' through!" It's a similar sentiment to that often expressed in the spirituals: "Soon I will be done with the troubles of the world. . . . Goin' home to be with God"; "Swing low, sweet chariot, comin' for to carry me home." Focus on the word *home*. Here, it doesn't refer to that warm place of acceptance, peace, and space to do as one pleases; rather, the longing is for something more than a comfortable residence as important as home is in this sense. The longing in these words is for a country, a home*land*—not just a place where an *individual* is comfortable and at peace, but a country—wherein, as far as we can see in every direction, everyone shares the kind of protected and cared-for feeling we all desire in our abode.

The writer of Hebrews wrote of people of God who were searching for a homeland in which their faith could be fulfilled, in which all the promises of God could be claimed in full. This would necessitate the absence of evil and spiritual distraction. Such a place was in their hearts and dreams, but they wanted a tangible expression of it.

Our writer has created a literary "faith hall of fame," a recalling of those who were known for their great faith though the full rewards of their faith were not realized on earth. Let that latter phrase be emphasized: *though the full rewards of their faith were not realized on earth*. The initial subjects in this faith hall of fame are Abel, Enoch,

Noah, Abraham, and Sarah. The values by which each of these lived and acted revealed that they were not caught up in or bound by the perspective of nonfaith. Even on earth they were living according to the standards of a heavenly country which, at best, they could barely glimpse.

Do you remember the story of Cain and Abel? When they were adults, these first two children of Adam and Eve had developed personalities and habits which were in sharp contrast—no consolation, but good reading for parents who marvel and moan at how differently the children they thought similarly reared turn out to be. The firstborn was Cain, and he became a farmer. The secondborn was Abel, and he became a shepherd. Only two professions in the world, and the sons take different paths! Even though Adam and Eve had been sent out of the Garden of Eden for their respective acts of disobeying God, they apparently had kept up the religious dimension of their lives. Both Cain and Abel knew that at harvesttime, an offering to the Lord was in order. Cain brought some of his crops as his offering; Abel brought the first lamb born in his flock of sheep. God was pleased with Abel's offering and not Cain's; obviously God's response had to do with Abel's desire to bring his best and Cain's tokenism. Jealous because of God's praise of Abel's faithfulness, Cain kills Abel.

Here is the writer of Hebrews using dead Abel as an example for others who would be faithful to God, and we think, as did the original readers, no doubt, "Are there any examples of people who were faithful and lived to tell about it?" What is Abel doing in this roll call of God's faithful anyway? Our writer explains that it was because of Abel's faith that he "offered God a better sacrifice than Cain" and that, though Abel is dead, "he still speaks by faith" (11:4, *The Jerusalem Bible*). Charles Trentham commented that Abel still speaks "as one whose faith in God has been rewarded and as one who is in the keeping of God forever."[1] The standards of the heavenly country establish that God's people give their best for God. That is why Abel is in this list; that is the sense in which he was reaching toward a homeland that he had not known on earth.

Enoch was one of the grandsons of Adam and the father of Methuselah who lived longer than any other person recorded in the Bible (969 years). Enoch lived a long time, too—365 years, but he was such a godly man that, one day, God just took him into heaven. The writer of Genesis tells us that Enoch "spent his life in fellowship with God" (5:24, GNB). What a eulogy! Do we know what it was about Enoch that pleased God so much? According to Hebrews 11, "It was because of his faith that Enoch was taken up and did not have to experience death. . . . It is impossible to please God without faith" (vv. 5-6, *The Jerusalem Bible*). Enoch was so sold to the way of life in the heavenly country that he was able to step right into it. Maybe we should see here that aside from Jesus of Nazareth no one on record ever did a better job of living according to a heavenly way of life on earth than Enoch did. Even though he was here a long time, this world was not his home; he was neither fulfilled nor complete here. There was a better world for which he reached.

Then there was Noah who lived in a time of such prevailing corruption that he was the only good man God could find. God decided that the creation of the human race had been a colossal mistake so it was back to the drawing board. The story is that God decided to flood the whole earth and virtually start all over again. To protect this one good man, his family, and a sample of all that was good in the rest of creation, God tells Noah there will be a great flood. To be protected from it, he is going to have to build a gigantic houseboat. No one, Noah included, had ever heard of any such thing. But, Noah decided to do it. Maybe he was afraid not to do it. In Hebrews, the writer noted that Noah "felt a holy fear and built an ark to save his family." Because his eyes were fixed on a greater world, he was able to follow God's instructions which made little sense to him and endure the taunts of people all around who kept insisting that they'd never heard of a houseboat or anything like it before. Actually, by Noah's faith and his focus on what transcended this world, our text explains that "the world was convicted" (v. 7, *The Jerusalem Bible*).

Not that he consciously passed judgment upon the world; that was not his to do. But every faithful confidence in God unconsciously and severely condemns the fretful lives of [those] who must establish their own security, obtain their own salvation, and work out their own destiny.[2]

You know Abram's (Abraham's) story, too. It was introduced in our Old Testament lesson.

It was by faith that Abraham obeyed the call to *set out* for a country that was the inheritance given to him and his descendants, and that *he set out* without knowing where he was going. By faith he arrived, *as a foreigner,* in the Promised Land, and lived there as if in a strange country, with Isaac and Jacob, who were heirs with him of the same promise. They lived there in tents while he looked forward to a city founded, designed and built by God (vv. 8-10, *The Jerusalem Bible*).

Abraham, literally, was in search of a new homeland on earth which, of course, was never fully realized. He was reaching for a city founded on the promises of God, a city whose builder and maker was God. That city, land, and country has never lasted upon this earth, but Abraham looked in faith.

Faith for Abraham was never a placid thing. It was a disturbing force compelling him to venture into the unseen. Faith that does not involve risk is not faith. True faith can never be based on conclusive evidence or upon carefully calculated profits. Faith acts upon that which is unseen, yet real. Faith feels the pull of the beyond.[3]

Talk about operating on other worldly standards, look at Sarah.

It was equally by faith that Sarah, in spite of being past the age, was made able to conceive, because she believed that [God] who had made the promise would be faithful to it. Because of this, there came from one man, and one who was already as good as dead himself [no offense, Abraham!], *more descendants than could be counted, as many as the stars of heaven or the grains of sand on the seashore* (vv. 11-12, *The Jerusalem Bible*).

Of course, when Sarah first heard the news that she was going to have a child in her old age after never having been able to conceive, she laughed. The implication is that she laughed with some sense of skepticism at what she heard about God's promise from the angel.

Actually, Abraham laughed, too, and Frederick Beuchner points out that they are laughing

> at the idea of a baby's being born in the geriatric ward and Medicare's picking up the tab. They are laughing because the angel not only seems to believe it but seems to expect them to believe it too. They are laughing because with another part of themselves they know it would take a fool to believe. . . . They are laughing because if by some crazy chance it should just happen to come true, then they would really have something to laugh about.[4]

But don't let Abraham overshadow Sarah on this one. She's in the faith hall of fame on her own. She was a woman who, as much as any man, longed for a world where things could be just the way God said they could be without any reservations or stipulations, even if the prospects made her laugh.

Each of these notable persons lived by faith hoping for that which was unseen but promised; in one way or another, they were on pilgrimage looking for a homeland wherein their promises could be fulfilled.[5] Life at its very best is never whole this side of heaven. Even at the end of what we would all consider a full life well-lived, there remains unfinished business. Rarely, if ever, are all one's dreams realized and promises fulfilled on earth. We are gifted through the grace of God many times over and blessed so richly that we take our blessings for granted, but we will never be complete until we are at home with God. At the same time, we have pain that in this world is never absolutely relieved, questions that are never fully answered, grief that never goes away entirely, and a sense of inadequacy that is not put away with finality. These voids and others like them remain with us in this place through which we pass. As preoccupied as we can become with them, these burdens are not the absolute determinants of our quality of life in the present or the future. Do you remember another of the old spirituals?

> I'm just a poor, wayfaring stranger,
>   A trav'ling through this world of woe;
> But there's no sickness, no toil or danger,
>   In that bright world to which I go . . .

I'm just a going over Jordan, . . .
I'm just a going over home.[6]

The singer is looking for her home; she knows that this world isn't it, and she knows she is, in some way, heading toward it. That is our song, too; it was the song of the women and men of faith who inspired the writer of our New Testament lesson. They were in search of their true homeland, and they knew "they were only strangers and nomads on earth" (v. 14, *The Jerusalem Bible*). Strangers and nomads, foreigners and refugees, and exiles are what they were; such is what we are. "In our own world of strife, of corrupt institutions and broken lives, of competitive greed and concentrated power, we, as men and women of faith, are strangers and exiles. This is not our home."[7]

Abraham and all the rest of these who were exemplary in their faith, desire to reach for a better world, and real homeland were made strangers and wanderers by the promise of God. They "could not settle down and make terms with things as they were. The patriarchs were condemned by their faith to accept their destiny in the distant future. This is the perennial burden of faith."[8]

The kind of perspective which allows or requires us to look beyond the disappointments and the imperfections of the present to a time and place where all these are somehow put away is a perspective of faith. Someone has spoken of the fact of human incompleteness against God's faithfulness.[9] If we can believe that there will be some point when all of God's promises to His people will be fully delivered and a utopian moment when they will be realized in full, then we are caught up in the power of faith. After all, we have heard the writer of Hebrews setting this entire discussion in the context of faith: "Only faith can guarantee the blessings that we hope for, or prove the existence of the realities that at present remain unseen" (v. 1, *The Jerusalem Bible*). We may know this first verse of Hebrews 11 in the *King James Version* rendering: "Now faith is the substance of things hoped for, the evidence of things not seen." The word we have translated *substance* suggests a foundation; faith, then, is the foundation of the Christian life and the Christian pilgrimage.[10]

We are on a pilgrimage toward our heavenly home and the new

Jerusalem, and that focus will carry us through much that is unpleasant, destructive, debilitating, and nonsensical about the life that is ours in this world. That is comforting; it is hopeful. Yet, while our focus is ever beyond the immediate, we must be careful not to make the obvious mistake; we must be careful not to write off the present as insignificant. This world with all its imperfections is still our place for a time, and in our search for our homeland we still work to leave the places through which we travel touched by the goodness and graciousness of God which pull us toward our goal. In spite of the fact that we know better, we live in this world—and pour ourselves into making it heavenly—as if it is all we have. That is precisely the way we find our way to the homeland God has built for us over there. God leads us all the way!

Notes

1. Charles Trentham, "Hebrews" in *The Broadman Bible Commentary,* vol. 12 (Nashville: Broadman Press, 1972), 80.

2. J. Harry Cotton, "The Epistle to the Hebrews," *The Interpreter's Bible,* vol. 11 (Nashville: Abingdon, 1955), 724.

3. Trentham, 81.

4. *Telling the Truth: The Gospel as Tragedy, Comedy & Fairy Tale* (New York: Harper & Row, 1977), 50.

5. R. Alan Culpepper, "A Superior Faith: Hebrews 10:19—12:2," *Review and Expositor,* Spring 1985, 384.

6. "I'm Just a Poor, Wayfaring Stranger," *Hymn for the Living Church* (Carol Stream: Hope, 1978), 540.

7. Cotton, 728.

8. Ibid.

9. Ibid.

10. Trentham, 78.

13
Demanding a Blessing

(Genesis 32:3-8,22-30; Luke 18:1-8)

We are not immune from pain and struggle. We can't ignore crisis and tragedy, and we can't escape them. They're with us from time to time and will continue to be, so what do we do with them?

Some of us have a quick answer. We give in right away. No contest. Tragedy wins, and we lose. The best we hope for ourselves in such situations is to be able to run away as quickly as we can from what has harmed us to where we can nurse our wounds. Perhaps reacting in any other way has never even occurred to some of us. Giving up is the most natural response because we are absolutely uncertain that there is anywhere or anyone to whom we can turn, and we're quite sure that we can't take the pain alone.

That may be part of the problem. While we can turn to others for comfort and solace in our pain, others cannot endure our pain for us. There is much that is unpleasant in life which, in terms of direct contact, we have to bear alone. How often have we wished we could suffer in place of someone we love? But we cannot, and this assuredly is one of the reasons we all feel utterly alone at times. Facing our own illness, tragedy, economic devastation, or family crisis leaves us frightened and feeling isolated—the one and only afflicted by a capricious turn of cruel nature.

In Stephen Crane's story, "The Open Boat," four men in a lifeboat are rowing along in the middle of nowhere after the steamer on which they were traveling sank. They are not certain they will make it out of this situation alive. Should they keep trying, though, in spite of their frustration, fear, and fatigue? Or should they be realistic and simply give up? The narrator of the story points this out

when it occurs to a man that nature does not regard him as important, and that she feels she would not maim the universe by disposing of him.

> He at first wishes to throw bricks at the temple, and he hates
> deeply the fact that there are no bricks and no temples. Any visible
> expression of nature would surely be pelleted with his jeers.
>
> Then, if there be no tangible thing to hoot he feels, perhaps, the
> desire to confront a personification and indulge in pleas, bowed to
> one knee, and with hands supplicant, saying: "Yes, but I love myself."
>
> A high cold star on a winter's night is the word he feels that she
> says to him. Thereafter, he knows the pathos of his situation.[1]

Sometimes, for us, when we are not able to think clearly, God and
nature are the same entity. We feel assaulted and, at the same time,
abandoned by God. Talk about pathos! That high, cold star, that
remote, silent object is, in our reckoning, none other than God. But
is it ever true that God assaults us and then leaves us hurting? Is it
ever true that God assaults us at all?

Jacob believed he wrestled with God. The encounter in question came about after a long series of strangely interconnected
events. You, no doubt, remember many of them. We all recall Jacob's
tricking his twin brother, Esau, out of the family birthright which
meant more material possessions and prestige—normally for the
oldest son in the family. We all probably remember the story of Jacob
stealing Esau's blessing from his nearly-blind father Isaac by some
skillful planning and playacting. We remember these stories, but we
may not recall what Esau did when what had happened finally
dawned upon him. He decided to kill his conniving brother, Jacob
(Gen. 27:41). The news of Esau's intention sent Jacob running.

The Old Testament story picks up many years later. The brothers haven't seen each other in years. By this time, both are married
and heads of their own households. They seem to have done well for
themselves.

Evidently, Jacob gets to the point in his life at which he is reflective enough to have appropriate regret for some of the many ways he
had taken advantage of people, and right at the top of the list is his

brother, Esau. He finds out that Esau is living in the land of Seir, and he sends some of his servants ahead, asking if it might be possible to heal old wounds. Esau doesn't answer. He simply tells the servants to inform Jacob that he and 400 of his men will be coming to meet him to talk about old times. Jacob, of course, was terrified—and rightly so. However, Jacob is tired of running. Still, he doesn't want to lose at Esau's hand everything he's worked so hard to accumulate all these years, so he divides his people and his possessions into two groups so the most he can lose is half of it all.

From the part of his estate which he had kept close by, Jacob designated a generous gift for his brother and went to great effort to arrange how the gift would be presented—well before Esau could actually see Jacob.

The half of Jacob's estate which he had kept for easy access and his family was sent across the Jabbok ford. As a precaution against meeting Esau face to face, Jacob brought up the rear and for some reason trailed behind a good bit. Alone on this side of the Jabbok, Jacob had the experience of his life. There wasn't a fun thing about it. "Jacob was left alone. And there was one that wrestled with him until daybreak" (Gen. 32:24, *The Jerusalem Bible*). He may have thought for a moment that Esau had come up on his blind side, but with a moment's reflection, he became convinced otherwise. Actually, when Esau and his 400 men finally did reach Jacob, they came in peace; Esau came for reconciliation. However, that was later.

For the moment, Jacob is left alone in the wilderness; that is where he wrestled with his mysterious opponent. He was literally alone in that he was in the darkness without a single family member or servant around. To make it worse, the inescapable focus of his thoughts was his crooked pattern of relating to people; he could not stop thinking about the wrongs of his life, and that was a great crisis for Jacob. There was loneliness and despair in the face of his failings. And, to heighten all the tension, he wasn't sure he'd live through the night. The last he'd heard from Esau, his brother had planned to kill him. Jacob, no doubt, believed that God had brought all of this to him and God was trying to tell him something as it were.

We are not surprised, then, to learn that Jacob takes the one

with whom he wrestles in the night to be none other than God.
Now, don't write off Jacob as a crackpot, because isn't that precisely
our conclusion much of the time? Alone and in the darkness, facing
crisis of some sort, don't we come to think that God is behind it all?
That in the struggle, God Himself is combating us? Haven't many of
us been convinced, at one time or another, that God has it in for us?
Or at least that God could prevent our pain if God only cared
enough about us? Our perceptions are distorted. God is *the* Advo-
cate for the suffering and downtrodden in our world.

Do you remember Jesus' parable about the widow who kept
demanding justice from a callous judge? Time after time he put her
off, but she kept appealing; and finally the judge said to himself,
"Though I have neither reverence for God nor regard for [human-
ity], yet because this woman annoys me I will give her justice, lest
by her continual coming she wear me out" (Luke 18:4-5, GNB). And
Jesus' comment on this story was: "Will not God see justice done to
[God's] elect who are crying unto [God] day and night, even if
[God] seems to delay helping them?" (vv. 7-8, GNB). There is a kind
of divine justice in having good come out of evil. The parable says
that those who seek justice of whatever sort will, ultimately, experience it.

Jacob was seeking justice; he wanted the just opportunity of
seeing things in his life made as right as he could make them. The
mysterious antagonist who represented for him both his enemies
and his God might very well end Jacob's life in a cul de sac in which
he did not want to end it. Jacob was determined to fight for all he
was worth to prevent that; he would fight his crisis and demand a
blessing of it. He would demand a blessing even from what caused
his pain. Add to all the pain Jacob had already known in his life—all
the rejection, all the fear, all the guilt—add to these the pain of the
struggle itself. When the one with whom Jacob wrestled saw that
Jacob could not be defeated at this time and in this manner, he struck
Jacob "in the socket of his hip, and Jacob's hip was dislocated as he
wrestled" (Gen. 32:25, *The Jerusalem Bible*). This was no dream.
Jacob would limp the rest of his life.

The hurts in our lives are that severe; they can leave marks of battle on us for the rest of our days on this earth. We very well may go on living and trying to make the most of what we have to work with, but we may walk with a slight limp as long as we try to walk at all. Faith healers—more than Jesus—have made us think we can get on after a serious wound without pain from time to time.

Could you have imagined how *any* good could have come to anyone who lived in the aftermath of San Francisco's 1989 earthquake? The tragedy was unspeakable! We will not minimize that or try to rationalize the irreplaceable losses of life and well-being in any sense. Didn't it strike you as remarkable that survivors didn't just pick up and get out of there? In contrast to what we might expect, National Public Radio reporters focused in on the immediate sense of community and helpfulness put to work by those who lived through this catastrophe. Rescue efforts, formal and informal, by professionals and persons on the street, began instantly and remained relentless for days and weeks. Talk of rebuilding and learning from structural mistakes began at once. The people were demanding a blessing from the godless destruction.

The question we have to ask ourselves is, can we receive a blessing out of our struggle? Are we willing to demand one? Is life worth enough to us that we will not let it be destroyed even by the aggressive assault of tragedy and grief, personal failings and loss of prestige, and lingering threats to well-being and religious doubting? Will we be brave enough in the struggle with these to face them head on, and will we refuse to let them go until even these expressions of evil add something positive to our lives? Here is the utter paradox of Jacob's story and ours. Its truth only works in God's economy: God is not the author of evil, but God, and only God, can help us wring something beneficial out of what has sought to destroy us. I can't tell you precisely how it's done; each of us can only know in the heat of the struggle.

Note

1. Stephen Crane, "The Open Boat," *The Norton Anthology of American Literature*, vol. 2, 2nd ed. (New York: Norton and Co., 1979), 735.

14
Staying with It

(Ruth 1:1-18; John 8:31-38)

It's a mobile society we live in. We're always busy, ever on the go, and not just in our activities but in our agility with moving through and beyond relationships and responsibilities which no longer suit us. The truth is, many of us have become suspicious or frightened of long-term commitments of any kind.

In contrast with the traditional emphasis we have placed on marriage for a lifetime, barring the untimely death of a spouse, of course, I heard a radio ad the other day that probably sizes us up pretty well. The mellow female voice was trying to sell bridal accessories, and her summary statement was something like: "You only get married for the first time once."

Haven't you noticed the gradual changes in our wedding ceremonies? The minister used to ask the bride and the groom, "Are you willing to be faithful and love through thick and thin as long as you both shall live?" Now there's such a high percentage of divorce—I've heard recently that it's just under 50 percent—that "so long as you both shall live" has been dropped, and the couple is now asked in essence if they are willing to be faithful to each other and love one another through thick and thin only as long as such an arrangement seems convenient. We are much more at ease these days breaking marital and relational commitments than we used to be.

This is true professionally as well. I grew up in a household, as did many of you, where the dedication of my parents to their jobs was an evidently unshakable fact of life. My father drove thirty miles every day each way to his job—still does; he's been doing it for some thirty-five years now. He was committed to his job and whatever it took to do the job well. He tried to instill those values in me by saying, "Once you tell somebody you're going to do something you do it."

Dad encouraged me to take a job bagging groceries when I was sixteen years old. I didn't mind bagging the groceries. What I hated were the extra jobs—the tasks we were assigned when there weren't rushes at checkout lines—like scraping chewing gum off the floors and disposing of spoiled dairy products. I once had a run-in with the owner, and I quit. I was unemployed for about eight hours—from the morning I quit until my father found out what had happened. He called the store owner, apologized for me, and asked for my second chance which I didn't want. "Why did I have to work for such an unjust man," I demanded.

Dad's reason was simple: "Because you took the job." So I went back to work that night thinking that I would be bagging groceries for the rest of my career, since I had unwittingly had taken the job and thereby irrevocably chosen my life's profession at age sixteen.

It's a different world now. Society has come to expect a sizable number of people *not* to stick with the same job or even the same career over time. Many people change careers one or more times in their lives and, to do so, go through all the retooling and retraining required. In a sense, such new freedom and opportunity is great for us. If we make a mistake in choosing our initial career or for circumstances beyond our control we lose the opportunity to practice that initial career, we aren't stuck for life. Also, if our interests change or there is the opportunity for a new challenge, we are often able to respond to it. Thank goodness for options! But, don't we also see, with this new freedom to rechoose careers, unhappy or confused people who use it as an excuse not to buckle down and make the most of what may be quite a good career? People who are unhappy or confused about life in general trying to change all the externals to achieve some level of happiness without getting to the heart of their internal difficulty?

I have special concern about "church hoppers." You know what church hoppers are, don't you? They are those who jump from church to church. They are always looking for something no church can provide—perfect programs and people who always see and do things their way. When a church can no longer provide this—and none can consistently—the church hopper moves on. She or he has no concern for a long-term contribution to a single church family and, thus, never really feels a part of any place. It's tragic. Many of these people are high-energy types who put much of themselves into serving wherever they happen to be members at a given time, but they never feel like they get back what they want for serving so diligently. Certainly no church can be all things to all people, and there is, justifiably, some people who come into a church without knowing it well and find out that it's not the right church for them. These people *ought* to move on. However, those who move on because of a legitimate ideological difference with a local congregation are not the church hoppers who keep moving from congregation to congregation because none of the churches can please them in every respect.

In each of these examples, I'm simply suggesting that it's easier these days *not* to take as seriously as we might much that is essentially positive in our lives because of the lure of other options which may seem to offer something we're not getting with our present arrangement—whatever it is. We become interested in change for change's sake, and in the process we can become caught up in forgetting about the validity of long-term commitments of all sorts. In fact, rapid and frequent changes become idealized to us. We admire those who do well in simple, shallow, short-term relationships. We are envious of those who somehow keep themselves from getting tangled up in the tentacles of tradition.

We're talking about the positive values of persistence and perseverance, and Ruth has become a prototype for the person who is willing to stay with it and stick it out. Ruth's proverbial persistence, unfortunately, is set against tragedy. The historical period is some time between the settlement of the Israelite tribes in the promised land and the beginning of the Israelite kingdom with the appointment of Saul as first king. It was a period for Israel of both war and drought which devastated the people.[1] No doubt these had contributed to the famine in much of the land, including Bethlehem where

Elimelech lived with his wife, Naomi, and their two sons, Mahlon and Chilion. The famine forced this family—and, no doubt, many others—to leave Judah in search of more food and better times. Their travels took them across the Jordan River and into the promising country of Moab where they settled. They did not leave tragedy behind them in Bethlehem. Within a ten-year period, Elimelech died, as did both of the sons. Mahlon and Chilion had married Moabite women during this time, who joined their mother-in-law, Naomi, as widows. Orpah and Ruth were mourning, too. They weren't simply mourning their losses of mates; they were mourning their return to the level of radical vulnerability and societal insignificance. Generally, a woman had status only when she was in clear relationship with a man—typically father, brother, uncle, husband, or brother-in-law. Among other factors, women were not able to support themselves, and they were, therefore, dependent on men to provide for them. In fact, as Evelyn and Frank Stagg point out in their book *Woman in the World of Jesus,* widows couldn't even inherit in their own right. "A childless widow had two options: remaining in her husband's family through levirate marriage or returning to her father."[2]

> In the event of the husband's death, the woman stayed in the new family [assuming that there was some male head of family], either as the mother of children, or being passed to another son [previously a brother-in-law to her] in the institution of levirate marriage. In such a system, women had no direct access to power or decision making.[3]

Even the usual limited options were further restricted for these three women: Naomi, Orpah, and Ruth. We don't know what, after all these years, was the status of Elimelech's family and Naomi's relationship to it. Her age precluded a new marriage anyway. Now childless and likely beyond childbearing years, none of her brothers-in-law would have wanted her. To make it worse, she was far away from her homeland. As for Orpah and Ruth, both childless, they may have had the option of returning to their fathers' homes in Moab, but there were no brothers-in-law. For the time, the best option seemed to be for them to remain with Naomi.

Naomi had heard that things were better in Judah—that times

were peaceful and rains had alleviated the drought and famine. People there were praising God for the good He had brought to them. Naomi's plan was to head back to Bethlehem. As she set out on her journey, Ruth and Orpah were traveling with her. Apparently, en route, Naomi became convinced that her young daughters-in-law would be better off to stay in Moab, each with her mother. She decided to send them back. "Go back, each of you to her mother's house. May Yahweh be kind to you as you have been to those who have died and to me. Yahweh grant that you find rest, each of you, in the house of a husband" (Ruth 1:8-9, *The Jerusalem Bible*).

Orpah and Ruth were more likely to find husbands in Moab than in Judah. And while Naomi, no doubt, would have been comforted a great deal by the presence of her daughters-in-law, she unselfishly wanted what was best for them. She kissed them, and in a most poignant scene, the younger women cried, protesting out of their loyalty to someone whom they obviously loved a great deal. With reluctant reason, Naomi explains:

> You must return, my daughters; why come with me? Have I any more sons in my womb to make husbands for you? Return my daughters, go, for I am too old now to marry again. Even if I said there is still hope for me, even if I were to have a husband this very night and bear sons, would you be prepared to wait until they were grown up? (vv. 11-13, *The Jerusalem Bible*).

Naomi couldn't hold it in any longer. She believed that all the tragedy had come to her and her loved ones because of God's anger. It was a common way to respond to bad news, still is, and it heightens the tragedy. To think that in addition to the grief of losing loved ones God is punishing you in ways that can't be taken back must be overpowering. How grateful we should be for a newer and clearer revelation of God than that. Still, Naomi only had what was known to her.

Caught up in familial, practical, and theological grieving, they began to weep aloud again. Orpah kissed Naomi and, for very good reasons, turned back to Moab; maybe they would never see one another again. "But Ruth clung to Naomi" (v. 14, author).

Naomi pressed Ruth one more time: "Go back to your people

and your gods as Orpah has done" (v. 15, author). Ruth was determined that she would not leave Naomi, and her explanation is preserved for us in a memorable, poetic statement. Ruth said to Naomi:

> Do not press me to leave you and
> to turn back from your company, for
> wherever you go, I will go,
> wherever you live, I will live.
> Your people shall be my people,
> and your God, my God.
> Wherever you die, I will die
> and there I will be buried.
> May Yahweh do this thing to me
> and more also,
> if even death should come between us!
> (vv. 16-17, *The Jerusalem Bible*).

This is beautiful. It says, in essence, that in a devoted relationship my whole life will be intertwined with yours. Where you are, there I want to be. People to whom you relate, I will relate. As you honor God, so will I honor God. And, then, with an oath which we cannot understand, Ruth says may God punish me if anything short of death separates us or comes between us. That's some kind of determination!

There are all kinds of things that can come between us and those we love. We have to work hard, very hard, not to let changing attitudes and differing needs damage a commitment of love. Leave the punishment of the God issue aside. It's still a great act of devotion to think in terms of sharing life with another over the long haul and to speak of the absolute seriousness of one's intention.

Incidentally, both the daughters-in-law made good decisions here. Orpah is not to be criticized for her decision to take Naomi's advice and try to make a life for herself in Moab. Orpah was certainly willing to give up many opportunities for her future and go with Naomi if that was what Naomi thought best. Orpah may be the perfect example of the person who chooses not to follow through with an initial commitment for valid reasons. She does not walk away from the life in which she was originally involved with any kind of frivolity or carelessness. Having been brought up to revere and respect members of the household of her husband, she had made it quite clear that she would care for the mother of her now-deceased husband. There was a legitimate opportunity to try a new way of life so she walks back to Moab with Naomi's blessing and our blessing as well. Orpah is certainly not the indifferent, rootless person who just can't or won't stay with a responsibility. Orpah is a heroine in her own right.

Ruth was the one who stayed with a potentially difficult role and responsibility no matter what the consequences. We must applaud such loyalty, and let us also learn from it. Naomi saw that Ruth meant to go with her and stay with her—period—so she finally stopped pressing Ruth to go back to Moab, and Naomi accepted Ruth's expressions of devotion.

Ruth's decision at its heart was, no doubt, relational. A good part of the reason she was doing what she was doing was because of her devotion to Naomi. There was something in Ruth that wouldn't quit. She was willing to stay with the course she had chosen—not in a negatively stubborn way, not in a closed-minded way, or not in a way to prove that she is always right in everything she does. She had confidence that she could receive a blessing out of what is less than perfect. And, after all, dear friends, what position, relationship, church, or team is perfect? If we leave behind responsibilities and people because we experience them as imperfect, where, then, will we turn?

Ruth does teach us much about the importance of staying with it. I can't help believing that this is an important word for many of us today. Some of us today are thinking about giving up on some relationship or other arrangement which we don't have to give up on. We've already decided that we're not going to persevere. We're ready to walk away, not for any of the good reasons to cut it short. Don't give up on your marriage. Don't give up on your child. Don't give up on your education. Don't give up on your job. Don't give up on your therapy. Don't give up on your rehabilitation. Don't give up on your moral standards. Don't give up on yourself. Don't give up on life.

We can apply what we learn from Ruth to several areas in our lives, and we mustn't forget about applying it to our faith. That is what Jesus is getting at in His words from John's Gospel. Jesus said to the Jews who had declared faith in Him: "If you continue in my word, you are truly my disciples, and you will know the truth and the truth will make you free" (John 8:31-32, RSV).

"If you continue in my word," He says, *if you stay with it*—your Christian commitment, that is—you are truly My disciples. You will know the truth about life and faith, and this truth will make you free—not running around changing all the externals any time you feel trapped or displeased in a responsibility. In so many ways, only by staying with it can we find our faith and the efforts of our lives fulfilled.

Notes

1. J. Hardee Kennedy, "Ruth" in *The Broadman Bible Commentary,* (Nashville: Broadman Press, 1970), 467.

2. Evelyn and Frank Stagg, *Woman in the World of Jesus* (Nashville: Broadman Press, 1978), 25.

3. "Women," *Harper's Bible Dictionary* (San Francisco: Harper and Row, 1985), 1138.

15
One God for All People

(Ephesians 3:1-13; Isaiah 11:1-9)

It's rather flattering, isn't it, to be in some group which seems to receive God's special favor? Correct or not, many people imagine that this is true of them. Some people say our nation is so favored. They measure "divine favoredness" by material prosperity and progress. We *are* a wealthy nation. We are a free nation. We are a strong nation in many respects. We call ourselves a "Christian nation" which is problematic, since a large number of our citizens are, by conviction, non-Christian and, technically, only individuals and not institutions can be Christian. Nonetheless, we claim to be a Christian nation. In our pledge of allegiance, we refer to ourselves as "one nation under God." Our currency testifies that: "In God we trust." This should be adequate proof, shouldn't it, that God surely favors us over *all* the rest?

Some families who have a rather "smooth" life think God is bestowing special favor on them. They have money and jobs and believe that God helps those who help themselves. The children have never given their parents any real trouble, and the parents have never embarrassed the children through irresponsible behavior. Everyone gets along. They've experienced no tragedies, and they think, *We know how to please God*.

Some individuals think they have the corner on God's favor. Not long ago, an entertainer who sang songs about adultery received an award for her singing. As she tearfully accepted, she said, "God is *so* good." A Christian woman who believed that faith healing and the right kind of prayers were just the things said to an acquaintance who was dying from cancer, "The reason you can't get well is because there is unforgiven sin in your life which you ought to confess to God."

Now, who really is "in good" with God? Who are God's "special children"? Americans? Families for whom life is smooth? People who receive widely publicized honors and awards? Christians who are physically healthy? What about non-Americans? What about families with tons of pressures and problems and people who never get any fame, honor, or even a pat on the back? Are people who suffer illness and disease tenderly loved by God, too?

The earliest people with whom God had a "special relationship" were the Israelites. They were the "chosen" people of God. But, they misunderstood their "chosenness." Their status wasn't a position of favoritism. It was a position of service. The Jews didn't have exclusive rights to God. They were to take the benefits of their relationship with God and become a light to the nations. They were to point others to God. But, most often, it didn't work that way. Generally, as is true of most groups who have become proud of their chosenness, they became possessive and imagined that God was interested in them alone, working for them and not for other groups of people. In fact, the circle of who is regarded as "chosen ones" becomes smaller and smaller over time. When we organize a club or church, we act as if we want everybody to be a part of what we're going to do; it can be *that* important to us. In reality, though, we spend our greatest amount of energy dealing with those whom we do not regard as suited for our clique. We deal with our elitism by saying that barriers to participation can be overcome by any outsider who will agree with our point of view, denounce what we denounce, get a wardrobe up to par, and understand that people of color still have their place.

Strangely enough, and we almost never remember this, the earliest Christians were Jews like Jesus. The early Jewish Christians, too, misunderstood their position in relation to God. Jesus and Christianity ultimately were not only for the Jews; the early Jewish Christians didn't have exclusive rights either to God or this new revelation of God through Jesus. They were to take the benefits of their relationship with the Lord and become witnesses to all persons. They were to point others to Jesus Christ as Lord.

However, most often it didn't work that way. Generally, they became possessive, proud, and selfish as they imagined that Jesus was only for them. Anybody who wanted to become a Christian, they believed, had to become a Jew first. Well, of course! Anybody who doesn't do it our way is suspect.

Because of the brief earthly ministry of our Lord, this issue became more focused in Paul's ministry than in Jesus' ministry. When Paul wrote this Letter to the Ephesians, he was in jail. He was in jail when he wrote Ephesians for an unbelievable reason.

Paul, too, was a Jew. He had maintained his contact with the Jewish traditions and practices as long as there was no conflict with the implications of his faith in Jesus Christ. He had gone to the temple one day with two Gentile men; he had taken a couple of friends to worship with him, and he was accused of taking them further into the temple than they were supposed to go. The temple was set up in sections. Animals, Gentiles, and lepers could only go in a little way into a court called "The Court of the Gentiles." Jewish women could go a little further. Jewish men could go a little further still. Priests could go up to the holy of holies, but only the high priest could go all the way into the center of the temple. The holy of holies was where the presence of the living God was thought to dwell, and a high priest could go to the center only one time a year. Paul was accused of taking Gentiles beyond their rightful place, and he was put in jail for it.

Now, Paul stood in a unique relationship with God—no doubt. It was in his ministry that a place for Gentiles in the church was first proclaimed. That was no easy position to take. Anytime the church makes some expansive choice to include, at any level, those who have not been freely accepted the status quo is threatened.

In spite of our verbal commitment to reach out to others in Jesus' name, Christians have spent a good deal of our evangelistic and missionary energy trying to get persons not just to come to God in Christ, but to fit in with our system. We could reach out to people on the foreign mission or home mission field. We have not done much for people of different cultures who might get seriously interested in joining our churches and seeking the same kinds of leadership opportunities the rest of us want. You see, Paul wasn't proclaiming a Christian community in which people have their places and have churches built for them in their part of town. Paul didn't preach a "they-have-their-place" gospel; he preached a "come-in-and-sit-with-me" gospel.

Much of Christendom has yet to deal fairly with the issue of the equality of women and men before God, and, thus, many groups have yet to come to terms with women in ministry. Women don't have to keep their hair uncut and their heads covered in worship. They don't always have to be on one side or another of a husband to have status and a voice in the church. They don't always have to be on the front side of the pulpit either. We haven't fully believed or accepted it yet, but someone once summed up the whole matter: "At the foot of the cross, all are equal." When the church decides to move away from the foot of the cross of Jesus, it may be a great organization, but it is no longer the church of Jesus Christ.

The message of inclusivism burned deeply within Paul, and it colored all he said and did. He was bold enough to preach it. He was God's spokesperson for that hour. Notice that his place in God's plan didn't make him peerless or entitle him to any position of exclusivism.

If, in any way, our nation, church, or families have been blessed of God, this has not come because we have earned it or God likes us better than anyone else; it is for the purpose of greater service. That's the way things work in God's system. Any blessing or talent or special calling is not for the recipient's personal acclaim, to set her or him apart; it is for use in ministry to God's people—either those in the church or still outside the church. This means that if God has brought you through some dark valley like depression, alcoholism, or bereavement, your job is only half done when you rejoice and praise God for His gift. You haven't done what you need to do until you make yourself available to others who need help out of the same bondage from which you've been freed. All this implies that we refuse to see those groping in darkness—for whatever reason—as God-forsaken. No human being is or *ever has been* God-forsaken. We have repeatedly forsaken God, and God has repeatedly given us the freedom of our choices. God is not in the business of forsaking people—no matter what their plight—because of a divine love beyond our understanding.

The Jews and most of the early Jewish Christians thought the Gentiles were God-forsaken. Here were God's people busily involved in leaving people out and often saying that there simply could be no place for them in the churches. However, something else was revealed to Paul. To some extent this revelation was a mystery; no one before Paul had comprehended it fully. Certainly there had been hints here and there throughout Israel's history, but as God worked in Paul's life, all the hints began to be pulled together. As Paul saw these in light of Jesus Christ, the truth dawned upon him in a way no one else, to that point in time, had seen it. So, even though the facts were as old as creation, the truth was new to the world that Paul knew. It took Jesus and someone completely sold out to Him—namely the apostle Paul—to bring the mystery to light. That's why Paul calls it not just a "mystery," but the "mystery of Christ" (Eph. 3:4).

God is not an exclusive or private possession of any person, family, church, denomination, nation, or Christian. God is the God *of all people and for all people*. While there are many benefits which come to Christians, benefits which come to us as children of God, we cannot assume that God loves us while not loving those who differ from us. The fact of the matter is, God is not possessed by anyone. God possesses. God possesses those who allow Him to relate to them in personal relationship. That possibility is open to *everyone*. No one is excluded.

As Christianity began to spread throughout the first-century world, more Gentiles than Jews came under its banner. Not only was there a place for the Gentiles in the church, but, also in time, they championed the cause of Christianity. In God's eyes, Jews were not preferred over the Gentiles. So, Paul said to the early Jewish Christians, "the Gentiles are fellow heirs, members of the same body, and partakers of the promise in Christ Jesus through the gospel" (v. 6). Whatever the inheritance is, it will not be based on anyone's nationality or religious preference. Regardless of any other circumstance, the inheritance of abundant life is offered to every single one of those who choose a life of commitment to God.

There is a communal element to this fact. All of God's people are members of one body—the church, the body of Christ. We are all related to one another, dependent on one another, and involved with one another. We're all working toward the same goals, at least supposedly, so we're supportive and not divisive. Anyone who is not with us is in that position for one of two reasons—as far as I can tell. The person either does not know about the possibility of a personal relationship with God through Jesus Christ or does know and has consciously decided not to be a part of it.

If this assessment is true, there are some matters we need to straighten out. We are a part of the larger human family, and all of us are loved by God. Jesus gave His life so all of us might come to know God personally. If we have really heard the gospel then all of us who name Jesus Christ as Lord are *preoccupied* with helping others hear who haven't. One-time Archbishop of Canterbury, William Temple, expressed it simply: "The Church is . . . a minority in a world to be won for Christ."[1] That staggers us a bit; we don't like to think we're in a minority because we like to be in control.

Furthermore, there is no group within the Christian community who has the corner either on God or on truth. Today is a good day to remember that. Christians all over are considering our common calling and the mutual responsibilities we share. No one Christian group has it together so astoundingly more than any other. The different groups rightly have differing practices and theological emphases. The right group for you is the one in which a particular mix of practices and doctrinal concerns are most meaningful to you, make the most sense to you, and help you the most with celebrating the reality of the living God.

Your group, my group, or our group is not "better" or more important than another. I think one of the great sins of Christians in the modern world is our tendency toward separatism and elitism about our own little brand of the faith. By focusing so much on our theological position and its correctness over all the others, we have wasted an enormous amount of energy which has kept us from doing the deeds commanded of all Christians—matters which are commanded of us by God and are nonnegotiable. There is so much absolute clarity about matters of ministry and witness that there is more than we can keep up with; arrogance and infighting among Christian groups over what isn't clear or necessary to faith-expression is despicable and an absolute insult to the one God for all people.

Rather than spending time trying to determine who's right and who's wrong or who's more right than any other group, we move without delay to do the work clearly set out for all of God's people—to help make this world the place the prophet Isaiah envisioned. He spoke of a time when "the earth shall be full of the knowledge of the Lord as the waters cover the sea" (Isa. 11:9). Let that be what we, with all our sisters and brothers in Christ all over the world, work toward.

As we recommit ourselves to the tasks God has given us to do, we pause to give thanks also for our sisters and brothers in every expression of the Christian faith and all women and men in this world who join with us in naming Jesus Christ as Lord. We need each other.

We will not all agree on details and fine points of faith expression, and we do not need to. There will even continue to be major differences in our concerns and how we express our faith. Why should that be a problem? These people are like us—simply fortunate to have found an entry into the Christian family. We are not the leaders or even first among equals. Jesus Christ is the head of the family, and through Him we find our way—as do all the others—to the blessings of God. We all quickly find also that this family is a working family. When we come to grips with the reality that God truly is the one God for all people, even for all Christians, there's more to do than all of us can accomplish with our very best efforts! Let us go forth in the assurance of God's presence with us when we serve the Lord and with the knowledge that there is more support and love in the family in Christ than we have ever taken the time to see.

Note

1. Clyde E. Fant, Jr. and William M. Pinson, Jr., eds., *Centuries of Great Preaching* (Waco: Word, 1971), 195.

16
Mercifully Dealt With

(1 Timothy 1:12-17; Exodus 32:1,7-14)

Have you ever had any serious reflection about how loving parents can take in stride verbal abuse and other teenage acting out from their children? Have you ever wondered how, on the morning after you spouted out harshly and hatefully at your mother when she called your hand on an obvious violation of acceptable behavior, she could greet you with a smile and a kiss and an aggravatingly sincere, "I love you"? Haven't you wondered how, on the evening after you blessed out your father for telling you can't keep on doing something, he could show up on the tail end of a hard day at the office with tickets for the two of you to attend the football game you were dying to see? Or, after a whole season of adolescent rebellion and all kinds of reasons not to trust anymore, how can parents send a child to college to face a tough world as an adult with nothing *but* trust and goodwill? A mystery.

Many of us, I'm sure, have had on occasion some sense of distance between ourselves and God and some sense that at times in our lives that we have knowingly and continually violated God's will and openly rebelled in our own way against Him. Those memories cause us both sadness at how unnecessary and inappropriate such a way of life was as well as amazement that God kept on loving us and caring for us anyway. It's kind of staggering, isn't it?

One of the great fathers of the church, Saint Augustine, reflected on his life before relationship with God in his great devotional classic, *Confessions*. He described eloquently this dimension of God about which we're speaking. You see, before his dramatic conversion, Augustine had been openly a scoundrel with quite an appetite for sins of the flesh. In retrospect, he became convinced that even in his most clear-cut periods of self-alienation from God, in an absolutely pre-Christian condition, God was bringing him into certain situations which finally had a bearing on his opening himself to relationship with God. That's quite some faith, isn't it? In prayer Saint Augustine reflected:

> Is there any evil that is not found in my acts, or if not in my acts, in my words, or if not in my words, in my will? But you, O Lord, are good and merciful, and your right hand has had regard for the depth of my death, and from the very bottom of my heart it has emptied out an abyss of corruption. . . . I have not forgotten, nor will I keep silent concerning the sharpness of your scourge and the wonderful speed of your mercy.[1]

> I uttered sighs, and you gave ear to me. I wavered back and forth, and you guided me. I wandered upon the broad way of the world, but you did not forsake me.[2]

"You did not forsake me." That could be a part of our prayers to God as well. No matter how out of line we were or how far away from God, God did not forsake us. This is also the sentiment of the apostle Paul.

Paul once sat down to put on paper his thoughts about what serving Jesus Christ meant to him. When he did, his reflection caused him to take in the whole of his experience with God in Christ, from the beginning to the time that he recorded for Timothy.

Paul, like the rest of us who would be honest, had to begin with gratitude for God's mercy in sharp contrast with a leaning to be free of God. As he looked back over it all, downs and ups and all the in-between times as well, what Paul saw most clearly and unmistakably was the mercy of God evidenced in nearly everything this colorful apostle had seen and done both before and after he committed his life to God through Jesus Christ and endured in taking a stand for Jesus Christ in a pagan world.

You know, when somebody who has been through hard times or is in the midst of hard times talks about how good God is, I listen. The person has my attention. I feel the same way about someone who can own up to the fact that she or he hasn't always done her or his best for God. The test of God's goodness is not tied to how well things go for us and how successful we are, though I don't mean to suggest that you have to be either destitute or despicable to understand or own the prevalence of God's mercy in your life.

The point is: *when* do you say it? *When* can we testify to our belief in the goodness of God? Only when we're getting our way? Only during periods of obvious success or prosperity? Only when there are no questions that disturb us or keep us awake? Can we only testify to the goodness of God when our pathways are smooth? If so, what Paul is saying to his protege, Timothy, will not make sense to us. If there is not some space in our theological selves for a God who is working for our good, *especially* when times are trying and discouraging and we are running our hardest away from God, a hearing of Paul's word is not possible for us.

We have to understand that when Paul testified, "I give thanks to Christ Jesus our Lord, who has given me strength for my work" (1 Tim. 1:12*a*, GNB), he meant not strength to excel and command notice but strength to endure to get by, get up, and get at it another day. Paul, as arrogant as he could be, didn't believe he could have made it in *his* strength alone; rather, were it not for divine strength, strength from beyond himself, Paul would have run out of anything to offer. That divine strength came strictly because of God's mercy. Paul knew it. "I give thanks to Christ Jesus our Lord, who has given me strength for my work."

Against a background of Paul's religious fanaticism which brought about his greatest sins, paradoxically, he had persecuted the people of God in His name. If people didn't speak of God and worship Him in the way Paul envisioned as proper, he regarded them as godless. The God Paul served and upheld was angry and unforgiving. The only way of responding to people who didn't appease God the way that Paul thought was appropriate was to condemn them with punishment or even death. Yes, Paul had, on occasion, something to do with death sentences to the people of God, and the killings were in God's name. Can you imagine being so sure of your own conception of God that you would be willing to put to death or harm another person who found a different way of describing and relating to the same God?

We can understand the depth of Paul's gratitude when he said to Timothy: "I thank [Christ Jesus] for considering me worthy and appointing me to serve him, even though in the past I spoke evil of him and persecuted and insulted him" (vv. 12b-13). That may be just a sentence to some of us, but it was a profound confession of Paul which, undoubtedly, still ripped him apart.

Paul had done a bit of thinking about why he, of all people, had been called out by God to minister precisely to those whom he had hated and hurt. How could he ever earn the right to speak to people he had abused and the survivors of those whose deaths he had instigated? Maybe with sins bringing about less dire consequences than these particular sins of Paul, many of us often wonder about our worthiness to do what we are convinced God is calling us to do. What right have I to proclaim to you the good news of God in Jesus Christ whose high standards I have not always kept and whom I have assuredly hurt through my carelessness and willfulness? I assure you that my being here and speaking to you about the most important truths in your lives has much more to do with God than with me.

I somehow take it as an act of maturity to be able to consider the possibility that we might not actually deserve something of value, something of pivotal consequence, or some great privilege which has come to us by grace alone. In terms of our faith and awareness of God's great expressions of love, we can reflect, search, ponder, and study the matter for a lifetime and never find anything along the way that we did or could have done to earn all that God gives us.

The biblical writers at times just can't come to grips with a God who is so loving and forgiving. Especially in the Old Testament we find writers who explain God's grace in the face of human sinfulness as, actually, a change of God's mind. The gist is that God, when people sin, has to be angry, offended, and instantly in the process of planning punishment when, for some unknown reason that seems to have more to do with luck than love, God changes His mind. That's what happened one time when Moses was atop Mount Sinai in intimate conversation with God. Right in the middle of something Moses was saying, God interrupted: "Get back down there to those crazy people." Moses went down to find the Israelites in compromising positions. Before an idol (a golden calf), a meal had turned into an orgy. God said to Moses, "They've had it now. It's all over for these Israelites." However, Moses, who didn't want to be the last Israelite on earth, said to God, "OK, if you want to wipe out all the descendants of your great servants like Abraham, Isaac, and Jacob and you want all that energy you used in getting us out of Egypt to be wasted, go ahead. But, God, don't you think you should change your mind on this one?" (Ex. 32:1,7-14, author). And, behold, Moses changed God's mind. It doesn't appear that there was any love involved as far as the writer was concerned; it appears more evident that Moses was some great persuader—even of God!

Paul knew something more than this though he had been well-schooled in that Old Testament way of thinking about God. Paul surely wouldn't have claimed to understand it all, but the one thing he decided about was how this opportunity to be a minister of the good news of Jesus Christ had come to him: ". . . because I acted ignorantly in unbelief I was dealt with mercifully; the grace of our Lord was lavished upon me, with the faith and love which are ours in Christ Jesus" (1 Tim. 1:13-14, NEB).

In Paul's pain, he penned a great confession of faith. Having committed great wrongs in his life and suffered imprisonment and beating for his faith, Paul knew the meaning of God's grace and mercy. To this young man who would follow in Paul's footsteps as a preacher of the gospel, Paul wrote:

Here are words you may trust, words that merit full acceptance: "Christ Jesus came into the world to save sinners"; and among them I stand first. But I was mercifully dealt with for this very purpose, that Jesus Christ might find in me the first occasion for displaying all his patience, and that I might be typical of all who were in the future to have faith in him and gain eternal life (vv. 15-16, NEB).

Paul wants to be an example of what happens when one—even the foremost sinner—happens into the grace of God. Paul believed that if God could love him and use him, in spite of his overpowering sin, it could happen to anybody.

Do you ever think about the words as you sing that old hymn? "I stand amazed in the presence / Of Jesus the Nazarene, And wonder how he could love me, A sinner condemned unclean."[3] And have you ever seriously wondered the same thing?

This is the good news. God's grace reaches all of us—you, me, and everybody else. We know so, not because of how well things go for us, how saintly we are, how few sins are on our list, but because we know in our hearts how mercifully we have been dealt with. Our acts of rebellion have never broken the reality of God's stubborn love for us. Therefore, our failures cannot keep us either from the caring presence of God or from faithful service to those in need of the gospel and the Lord whom it proclaims. We cannot escape our responsibility to witness to God's faithfulness because of our unworthiness. Dear friends, because of God's mercy forgiveness is a reality, and we go forth, in a spirit of praise, to tell others of a God who has never forsaken us and who, even now, strengthens us day by day.

Notes

1. John K. Ryan, trans., *The Confessions of St. Augustine* (Garden City: Image Books, 1960), 205, 212-13.

2. Ibid., 140.

3. "I Stand Amazed in the Presence," *Baptist Hymnal* (Nashville: Convention Press, 1975), 63.

17
Great Reversals

(Isaiah 35:1-7; Matthew 11:2-6)

The prophet Isaiah spoke of a place and time of powerful contrasts. A desert dry and barren now in full bloom. Courage where there has been fear. People who were blind have their sight, and those who were deaf can hear. Someone once crippled is now with strong, healthy legs jumping like a deer, and words are pouring forth from vocal cords which had been unable to sound out any words. When we see the glory of the Lord, we see with it *great reversals*. We see the glory of the Lord when we see Jesus Christ.

Jesus isn't easily seen, is He? He's not easily seen in our lives, this world, or even at the time of year named in His honor. Listen, John the Baptist—Jesus' cousin, the first to acknowledge Jesus publicly as the Christ—began to wonder if he were correct in seeing the glory of God in Jesus of Nazareth which the prophets had promised. The evangelist who had proclaimed so confidently, "Behold, the Lamb of God who takes away the sin of the world!"(John 1:29) was now not so sure of that. In prison, this woolly, back-to-nature preacher began to waver in his confidence about Jesus' identity as the Christ and Messiah, and he sent his disciples to Jesus with a question reflecting his ambivalence: "Are you he who is to come, or shall we look for another?" (Matt. 11:3). If John the Baptist wasn't absolutely convinced of Jesus' identify as God's Son, how in the world can we be?

Here we are dealing with the ideas of the Messiah, messianic expectation, and a coming messianic age. What do these mean? Frank Stagg points out that the "Hebrew term *Messiah* means *anointed*. In the Old Testament it stands for *God's Anointed One*."[1]

When someone was anointed, he or she was being honored; God often honored people with a special calling to serve His people.

We mean precisely the same thing as Messiah when we use the Greek word *Christ*. Though there have always been variations of thought on the meaning of this word and concept, often there has been with Messiah the companion idea of "a new kind of future under the rule of God's Anointed."[2] In Jewish thought, the predominant understanding has been that the Messiah would be identifiable in the world because of the tremendous nationalistic and political advantages He would bring on behalf of the Jewish people. And, typically, this has been associated with the expectation that the Messiah would be a great warrior. Indeed, a warrior would be needed to liberate the often-persecuted Jews.

The Christian conviction is that Jesus is the Messiah, the Christ, but not the Messiah whom the Jews anticipated. This remains a primary difference between Christians and Jews today. *We* say that Jesus is the Christ, the Son of the living God, but what exactly do we mean by that? I suspect that many of us aren't all that concerned about any precise definition. Our theological conviction is clear enough to us, but most of us were drawn to Jesus in a personal, experiential sense before we made any effort to define Him. What does it mean for us to confess that Jesus is the Christ, Messiah, and God's Anointed?

We identify the man Jesus and the risen, living Lord as one in the same, and we further identify Jesus as divine—in genuine union with God. As God's Messiah or Anointed One, Jesus comes to bring God's kingdom and rule of love into being on earth. It all sounds good to us because we've had a few generations to reflect on the matter. How Jesus went about His mission and what He actually accomplished did not receive widespread approval by His contemporaries. Most of His fellow Jews couldn't get past the spiritual kingdom about which Jesus spoke when they wanted and had long anticipated an earthly, politically controlled kingdom that favored Jews. We all want a kingdom of God which favors us—our group, race, or denomination. The fact that Jesus wasn't especially successful in getting His message universally accepted during His earthly ministry caused many of His kinspeople to see Him as rather a failure—something absolutely unthinkable to the Jews in association with the Messiah. To them, the Messiah would be successful because He was the Messiah and with God-given power to demonstrate and enforce compliance with His universal and permanent liberation of the Jews.

Now if Jesus talks about the kingdom of God and a messianic age with universal application—that is, a kingdom made up of all who will come to God by faith in Jesus Christ—talks of this kingdom in nonpolitical and nonmaterialistic language, and envisions a kingdom begun but not fully established as yet—are we any more inclined to buy His message than were the first-century Jews? Aren't we more concerned about streets of gold and an honored place in God's cabinet than we are in individual and communal liberation? Aren't many of us more concerned, too, with a Messiah who lets us live to see our enemies drop dead than we are with a Messiah who, in His lifetime, never receives worldwide notice or acceptance? Do we think much of a would-be Messiah who lets one of the faithful rot away in some captivity, with a mad man threatening to execute Him while this Messiah is running around with the dregs of society?

John the Baptist is in jail not knowing exactly what will become of him. Queen Herodias hates him; she wants his head on a silver platter. John had said Jesus is *the one* who in God's power would liberate all the oppressed, and John felt like chief among the oppressed. He wanted to be liberated, but here was the one whom he had called the Christ evidently doing nothing to save him and, instead, spending time with a bunch of lowlifes who hadn't been involved in any significant way with Jesus. Neither had they shown much interest in what Jesus taught and valued. Don't you dare think John's concern about Jesus' identity was out of line!

John was asking, "So, Jesus, are you the coming one—the Anointed One, liberator, and Savior—or should we look for another? If you don't have enough power to liberate the one who gets hoarse every day trying to lead people to repent and turn to the God you say you represent, aren't we barking up the wrong tree?"

Jesus got the message. He heard John's question. And do you

know what Jesus sent back as an answer to John's inquiry? Not a neat and tidy, "Yes, I am He," or a heavyweight theological rationale. But a simple list of facts about His life which sounded something like what one of the prophets of old had said. Jesus responded to John's disciples, "Did you happen to notice anything different about me? Had it dawned on you what happens when I use my gifts? Blind people receive their sight. Lame people get up and walk. Lepers suddenly have the healthiest skin you'd ever want to see. The eyes of the deaf brighten up because they can hear what I say to them. Dead people are brought back to life, and poor people who only disgust society at large get seats of honor in my congregations? Tell your master, John, to help me figure out what all of this means!"

I asked a rabbi friend how the Jewish John the Baptist would have heard Jesus' explanation. He said, in essence, that Jesus' explanation would have been very weak to John because, with few exceptions, the very humility of Jesus in His association with these needy people was utterly incongruent with the Jewish idea of Messiah. The Messiah was expected to be about big-time power and military might, not about helping along the people society generally disregarded. Well, was Jesus the Messiah or not? Is Jesus the Messiah or not?

Advent isn't a time to shore up your systematic theology. Advent is a time to decide whether or not Jesus is God's Anointed by being honest about how He is active in your life and world. We cannot know whether Jesus is the Messiah, the Savior, if we try to decide purely on the basis of intellectual evidence. That's why Jesus couldn't give a simple answer to John's disciples. There are certain facts we must deal with in our hearts if we want to know about Jesus' role as Lord and Savior. Look for the great reversals where Jesus is said to be at work; look for drastic and unbelievable changes—healing and boundless hope—in the lives of people who have been touched by Him. These are the indications that God's rule of love is coming in our world through Jesus Christ. But this isn't enough.

Look for the great reversals in your own life. Can you find them? Do you have any indication that an oasis has sprung up when all you've known for as long as you can remember is desert? Have you ever had a glimpse of wholeness for yourself when you've been ready to give in to a lifetime of feeling broken? Has the silence of sorrow and sighing in your soul ever given way to joyful song? Have you ever been ransomed from the fear, sin, anxiety, and weakness which have held you captive?[3] If so, you know who Jesus is, and you also know that the search for God's Anointed One and the kind of world He is bringing stops with Jesus Christ.

Notes

1. Frank Stagg, *The Doctrine of Christ* (Nashville: Convention Press, 1984), 22.

2. Ibid.

3. Many of these images borrowed from Elizabeth Achtemeier in *Pulpit Digest,* November/December 1989, 89.

18
Shepherded

(Psalm 23; John 10:1-18)

Few people would fail to include Psalm 23 in their list of favorite biblical passages. For many it is at the top of their list. It has been used in all kinds of contexts through the centuries to comfort, encourage, and uplift persons like us who struggle with life. This beautiful psalm has served us well, as it continues to do. Whatever your need today, let Psalm 23 soothe you as it smooths the rough edges of your life.

This psalm has the power to soothe because it reminds us that the great God shepherds us; we are shepherded by the Almighty Himself. In God and the assurance of His love for us we can rest. It is a reality of life on which we can rely. When all else goes awry, as life often does, we have God to trust in, the God who lives, loves, and acts in our best interest.

Dr. John Durham points out that Psalm 23 is one of the several psalms in which the primary emphasis is trust in God. All of them, Psalm 23 included, radiate "a confidence in God's goodness, compassion, and unchanging love which will be neither deterred nor diminished."[1] We are shepherded by that kind of God. That is cause for relief and rejoicing!

The real emphasis in this psalm is on the central character, God—our Shepherd. God is the shepherd, and we are His sheep; God is the Good Shepherd. God is the Perfect Shepherd in providing for all of our needs—completely capable, reliable, and willing. The underlying question of the psalm is: Into whose hands can you place your life and be assured of such thorough care? The answer is: no one but God. This sort of life, relationship, and care come only from God, the Great Shepherd who shepherds us.

We are God's sheep. Incidentally, that is not the highest compliment paid to human beings in the biblical literature. We are not called sheep but are compared to them. Have you ever thought about what that means? Sheep are neither smart, fast, nor strong. They are rather helpless followers, largely dependent upon forces outside themselves for the satisfaction of even their most basic needs. Someone told me that sheep had been known to fall off a cliff because of going from one grazing patch to the next without awareness of any other factor.

The psalmist may not have complimented us by comparing us with sheep, but there is a great deal of accuracy in the comparison nonetheless. Most of us have even fallen off a "cliff" or two in our time.

As we look at the meaning of this inspiring psalm for our lives, I see several descriptions of what it means to be shepherded by God. It means *assurance* in who God is and what God will do in the sense we have already discussed. "The Lord is my shepherd" (v. 1).

Being shepherded by God means the provision of everything we need for accomplishment in our lives. "I shall not want" (v. 1). The psalmist literally means this in a very broad sense. He is thinking in terms of basic human needs like having food to eat and also in relation to emotional needs such as human dignity. In this sense, the Great Shepherd becomes the Great Host meeting our needs in the very presence of those who would not. There are enemies surrounding our lives—persons and forces—which would not have fed, clothed, or in any way provided for us. And almost, as if in a manner of holy "flaunting," God is setting the table for us right in the sight of those who oppose us (v. 3). But God wants to give us more than a snack. He's not giving us fast-food fare. The table God sets is a banquet, a spiritual feast with all the frills, because God intends to honor us. "The host . . . singles out the guest as honored and the feast as joyous by pouring scented oil upon the guest's head."[2] When Almighty God treats us so royally, then we can feel good about ourselves, and we humans have the need and the right to do just that.

When the psalmist realizes what God is doing for him, he is

overtaken, and he says worshipfully, in appreciative amazement: ". . . my cup runneth over" (v. 5). God's giving to us is unfathomable. In this moment thoughts of God's deeds could not be higher. The psalmist realizes that what he is experiencing in the present is exactly what he can expect in the future as God continues to shepherd him. "Surely goodness and mercy shall follow me all the days of my life" (v. 6). Goodness and mercy are from God and are such strong provisions for God's people; we can say they actually pursue us. When the pressures and evils of life are pressing in on us, God's mercy and goodness are stronger still; we don't always feel that. We can't verify that apart from retrospect, perhaps, but it is nevertheless true. One Scottish preacher talked about God's goodness and mercy as two fine collie dogs which see us safely home.[3]

Being shepherded by God means *rest* in the Lord. We're not talking about any sort of protection from the pitfalls which come to every human being. We're talking about confidence in God and in God's care of us *in spite of* what life may bring our way, *in spite of* how enemies may seek to hurt or destroy us. This confidence allows us to rest: "[the Shepherd] makes me lie down in green pastures . . . [and] leads me beside still waters . . ." (v. 2). If we do not find our rest in the Lord, where will we find it? There is no rest in our lives or peace for us apart from the inner calm which comes from God's presence and provisions. There are times to be disturbed, angry, and shocked—such as during the evening news. To have tension, anxiety, and ceaseless worry as a style of life is to destroy life. To have contentment and enjoyment as goals for living isn't some far-out hope or the invention of pop psychology; it is the possibility and reality when we follow our God. It is a reality in spite of outward circumstances. If God leads us there, that is the place to be. God does lead us beside the still waters.

Worry is one of the things I do best. Nonetheless, it is wrong. Why? Other than biblical mandates to this effect, I once read of the conclusions of J. Arthur Rank, an English motion picture producer. Rank, an outspoken Christian, decided to do all of his worrying on one day each week. When anything happened that gave him anxiety, he wrote it down and put it in his worry box. Each Wednesday he opened the box and found that most of the things which had disturbed him the past six days were already settled, and it would have been useless to worry about them.[4]

John Drescher reports that someone has estimated things people worry about fall into one of the following categories: 40 percent are things that never happen; 30 percent are things that can't be changed by all the worry in the world; 12 percent are needless health worries; 10 percent are petty miscellaneous worries; and 8 percent are real, legitimate worries. Conclusion? Most of us worry most of the time about things that never happen or can't be changed. Further, worry as a way of life becomes immoral because it harms us emotionally and physically and forces us to be poor stewards of our time and energy. It reveals a lack of faith in God's care of us and the integrity of God's promises.[5]

I cannot manufacture my own sense of well-being. I cannot control all the factors that have a bearing upon me. What I can claim, however, is that God who cares for you and me, will make everything work for our benefit in so far as benefit in this world is possible. When life is stripped to that level, and tragedy, misfortune, and sinfulness have made a present benefit impossible, I can still rest because God is sitting on the edge of the bed saying, "Rest now. I'm here with you."

All of this is closely related to the psalmist's conviction that he was protected by God. And in the sense I have described, being shepherded by God means *protection*. It's the protection from having to face life's most lifeless moments alone. We feel most "attacked" and "assaulted" by the lurking evils when no one stands with us to face them and ward off their effects. "Even though I walk through the valley of the shadow of death, I fear no evil; for thou art with me; thy rod and thy staff, they comfort me" (v. 4). The Shepherd is equipped to meet the forces which threaten the well-being of the sheep. God further protects us because ultimately God's will is triumphant; we are wounded in the battles of life, but not destroyed because where God is, life is.

Being shepherded by God means *renewal* in the Lord: "[the Shepherd] restores my soul" (v.3)—literally "refreshes my life."

Many times it's not the great battles with evil which steal our lives from us. It's the series of events which, if isolated, we might call "small things." The writer of the Song of Solomon called them "little foxes" and said: "Catch the foxes for us, The little foxes that are ruining the vineyards, While our vineyards are in blossom" (2:15).

The writer isn't particularly worried about the "big foxes" that could do tremendous and obvious harm; rather it's the little ones which do a little harm here and little harm there, almost unnoticed at any one time until, finally, the vineyard is ruined. Not one of these "small things" is major enough to be considered a crisis, but taken together they steal away the freshness of life and our ability to celebrate it. We don't realize it's seeping away, but we look up one day and suddenly our zest for life is gone. And what do we do? Often, we look erroneously for the kind of interest, satisfaction, and gratification we feel the need of in all kinds of places and in all kinds of experiences. But the psalmist looked in the right place—to God. It is God who renews life—makes it exciting, worth living, fresh. It isn't as if this is a once-in-a-lifetime or once-and-for-all renewal. We have an ongoing need for the renewal of life, for the restoring of our souls. Being shepherded by God obviously means *leadership for living*. Like sheep, we often lose our way. We need a reliable guide to follow, and God takes us where we need to be for our benefit and for the accomplishing of God's will in our lives: "[the Shepherd] leads me in paths of righteousness for [the Lord's] name's sake" (v. 3). God guides us in the right ways. What is right for us is determined by God's will and leadership.

> He leadeth me! O blessed tho't!
> O words with heav'nly comfort fraught!
> Whate'er I do, where'er I be,
> Still 'tis God's hand that leadeth me!
>
> He leadeth me, he leadeth me,
> By his own hand he leadeth me:
> His faithful foll'wer I would be,
> For by his hand he leadeth me.[6]

Finally, being shepherded by God means *the gift of God's presence*. This summarizes all the psalmist has sung (v. 6). For all the days of his life, he was confident that God would be his shepherd and host; he would not be out of the presence of his God. That is why he could pen this beautiful and eternal psalm. Whether in success or failure, in happiness or the fog of despair, the psalmist established a continuing relationship with the Great Shepherd—his leader, guide, Lord. When God becomes our Shepherd, an opportunity for which God pleads, these touching confessions become ours. You need that today, don't you?

Notes

1. John I. Durham, "Psalms" in *The Broadman Bible Commentary,* Vol. 4 (Nashville: Broadman Press, 1971), 216.

2. Ibid., 217.

3. *Review and Expositor,* Summer, 1984, 458.

4. *Pulpit Digest,* May—June 1983, 62.

5. Ibid.

6. Joseph H. Gilmore, "He Leadeth Me! O Blessed Thought," *Baptist Hymnal* (Nashville: Convention Press, 1975), 218.